**Nonaligned
Black
Africa**

This book is published for the Center on International Race Relations in their *Race and Nations Series.* The Center seeks the wider recognition of the role of race in international affairs, and through its research and teaching programs develops a systematic analysis of race in American foreign relations.

Nonaligned
Black
Africa

An International Subsystem

George W. Shepherd, Jr.

University of Denver

Heath Lexington Books
D. C. Heath and Company
Lexington, Massachusetts

**To Eduardo,
scholar-revolutionary,
whose ideals are
more alive among this
generation of students —
white and black —
than ever before.**

Contents

Preface   vii

Chapter 1   The Nonalignment Subsystem   1

Chapter 2   The Racial and Colonial Origins of African
                 Nonalignment   12

Chapter 3   Regional Rivalries and Caucuses Within The
                 African Subsystem   24

Chapter 4   White Intervention and Black African Reaction:
                 The Case of the Stanleyville Drop   38

Chapter 5   The Coming Confrontation Over Race: The
                 Rhodesian Case   50

Chapter 6   Southern African Liberation Movements: The
                 Turn To Violence   64

Chapter 7   The Community and The Commonwealth:
                 Toward New Patterns   76

Chapter 8   Nonaligned Black Africa and Communist Powers:
                 Bridge or Battleground?   92

Chapter 9   The United States and Nonaligned Black Africa   106

Chapter 10   Nonaligned Black Africa and World Peace   122

                    Index   145

                    About the Author   153

Preface

This book has been written with an eye to meeting a wide variety of interests in Africa. From the standpoint of the students of African politics, it provides a framework of systems analysis in which the multi-faceted interaction of the new African states can best be understood. For those who are interested primarily in policy issues, the book seeks to identify the origins of nonalignment and its significance in a world that has moved from a bipolar to a plural international system. The emergence of racial issues in world politics is especially significant in Africa where a black subsystem and a white dominance subsystem struggle for control.

Non-Africans have frequently been proven wrong in interpreting the African phenomenon, yet many Africans continue to take our works seriously. Perhaps the explanation and interpretation of the motives and policies of the great powers will prove to be of greatest interest to the African reader.

The baffled layman has also been a member of the silent audience as this book emerged. There is an important attentive elite in foreign policy matters in this country and elsewhere in the Western world. They struggle with a myriad of conflicting facts and events concerning areas of the world they know little about. They are not rewarded professionally for these efforts. Their main incentive is to create a better, more livable world. Specialists have a particular obligation in an open society to provide them with materials by which they can make wise judgments. Our profession has tended to drift away from this obligation and it is my hope that these pages partially make amends.

I cannot begin to list adequately the many credits deserved by others who have actively or unknowingly contributed to the ideas and materials I have used. The greatest debt is clearly to my students who have incessantly demanded greater clarification and better interpretation. Several research assistants, such as Akbarali Thobani, Cynthia Kahn, and Judith Ross, have, at various times, produced valuable information. *Africa Today* has been a resource of great assistance over the years, particularly the last four years in which I have served as editor. And Shirley Shepherd has taken time from her responsibilities as managing editor of *Africa Today* and housewife to assure accuracy and consistency in this book, as she has done so ably with all my publications.

The major ideas of this book have been discussed with several colleagues. They have often disagreed over the years, and their criticisms have been most helpful. Dennis Austin, Henry Bretton, Robert Good, I. William Zartman, W. A. E. Skurnik, Wilbert LeMelle, Tilden LeMelle, Muddathir Abdel Rahim, and Ali Mazrui have stimulated and criticized my thinking on the subject.

The earliest outlines of this book were started during two summers in Washington, D.C. at the Brookings Institution where my initial explorations into nonalignment and foreign policy were begun. Two research trips to Africa were made possible by the Rockefeller Foundation, and the Graduate School of International Studies has given me research leaves and financial assistance. Both have facilitated greatly the gathering of material and the writing of this book. During a year and a half at the University of Khartoum, I was provided facilities for research and travel in Africa that were of great help. During brief visits to various African universities and centers such as the University of Ghana and the University of Ibadan, librarians and professors too numerous to mention were most generous with their time and information. African officials and leaders who have patiently endured the enquiries of one more American professor, deserve special mention and the expression of a hope that their patience is not now exhausted.

George W. Shepherd, Jr.

Nonaligned
Black
Africa

1 The Nonalignment Subsystem

Nonalignment in world affairs is still a controversial and poorly understood concept despite its existence for two decades. Political leaders debate the proper content of nonalignment and political analysts question its nature and effect. Yet, its growing importance for the new states, particularly African, can scarcely be questioned. An overwhelming majority of the new African states have declared that their foreign policies are based upon nonalignment. More significantly, their behavior in the international system manifests this substantial new phenomenon.

Western views of nonalignment have been influenced by the assumption, widely held in political and academic circles, that only great powers determine the content of world politics. The popular realist view is that small powers of necessity fall within the spheres of interest of great powers. This perspective assumes a bipolar or at most, with China, a tripolar struggle. It assumes that small powers really are not independent but are subordinate to great powers.

A basic proposition of this work is that, because of radical changes in the international system, the new states are not necessarily subordinate to the great powers. Many have set independent courses that we generally describe as nonaligned, and, acting collectively, have created international subsystems. Moreover, various kinds of nonalignment and types of subsystems arise from the great differences in culture and situation. In both the theoretical and the actual senses, however, nonaligned subsystems have established themselves within the overall international system. Therefore, the content, effect, and direction of movement of these nonaligned states and systems should be clarified.

The emergence of the new African states from colonial subordination is in itself one of the most visible examples of the change in the international system. Yet the scope and significance of this change has not been grasped fully.

African and other nonaligned countries generally are discussed as a "third world", or as pawns in global great-power struggles. This view, strongly influenced by a Cold War interpretation of world politics, does not grasp the reality of an international system that is multipolar and nationally pluralistic. Changes in the international system of the sixties have reduced greatly the capability of great powers to control smaller powers and have increased the autonomy and importance of the small states.

The Western Bias

Much of the difficulty that great powers, especially the United States, have had in dealing effectively with new states and areas has arisen from their failure to see and accept the reality of nonaligned states and nonaligned subsystems. Theorists as well as practitioners reflect the interest and policies of their own countries. Thereby they have been slow to interpret the reality of these changes accurately.

The tendency of policy makers to treat areas as spheres of interest is most conspicuous in regional military systems such as SEATO and CENTO. The collapse of these alignment systems is proof that they did not reflect the aspirations of the nations they encompassed. Moreover, changing circumstances such as a transition from a bipolar to a multipolar world have undercut their utility.

Theorists have looked at Southeast Asia, the Middle East, and Africa as subordinate systems.[1] Each analyst has a different concept of the components of a subordinate system, yet each accepts as a basic proposition the assumption that the new states, as units, are not independent in the traditional European nation-state sense, but are dominated by great powers who influence development and control policy in a variety of ways. The contrary proposition of this book, is that Africa is developing a nonaligned subsystem within the global international system.

Not only does the nonalignment concept cut across the grain of the realist bipolar view of world affairs, but also it is a direct challenge to the status quo, particularly of the Western world. International trade, finance, and political systems were revised by Colonial powers after independence to maintain the close colonial relationship. Thus the West generally has regarded nonalignment as a threat to the post-colonial interests of the great powers. Not surprisingly, the West initially saw nonalignment as an immoral and pro-communist doctrine. Even economists and political scientists criticized the concept as spreading a dangerous wish for economic freedom from metropolitan relationships. The more revolutionary African proponents of industrialization and regional common markets frequently were discounted as premature or näive.

Those in the Western world preoccupied with the Cold War and an ideological interpretation of all phenomena have not been able to accept the reality of long-term independence of nonaligned states from communist expansionism. George Meany said in 1955, "Nehru and Tito are not neutral, they are aides and allies of communist imperialism — in fact and in effect if not in diplomatic verbiage."[2] Mr. Dulles was not the only Secretary of State to view nonaligned nations with suspicion; in 1960, Christian Herter accused Nkrumah at the United Nations of " . . . very definitely leaning toward the Soviet bloc."[3]

The Communist Bias

While the communist great powers lack historical relationship with nonaligned areas, ideologically they aspire to assimilate them, though the independence concept challenges this. Under Stalin, the Soviet Union denounced the "bourgeois notion" of neutralism frequently. And Khrushchev's ambiguous but famous remark "there are neutral nations but no neutral men" has become a rule of thumb for realists far beyond the communist world.

Thus, objective analysis has emerged slowly in the communist world as well as in the West. And policymakers face the difficult task of deciding what policies to pursue toward those who have challenged existing interpretations and interests.

These failures in the analysis of the international system and the nonalignment phenomenon in general may well be more than bias. As J.W. Burton suggests, the prevailing power-factors view of nation-states has a basic fallacy.[4] Perhaps we need a view of the life of nations based more upon their culture and function than their economic productivity and military technology, i.e., more Weberian than Marxian. How else can we explain the capacity of the Vietnamese to frustrate the power of "the mightiest nation on earth"?

The Nonaligned Bias

Leaders in the new states have many difficulties in defining and agreeing upon nonalignment. Their understanding of world affairs is limited by inexperience. They tend to exaggerate their power and independence. Frequently they do not understand the variety of forces that operate in different countries to produce various viewpoints and doctrines. Some African leaders sought an impossible African political union, trying to unite all Africa in common policies toward the outside world. They extended this idealistic view to the goals of disarmament and peaceful coexistence without fully understanding the nature of the ideological and historical-interest confrontation of the great powers. Their tendency to accept at face value communist-world statements of support for peace and self-determination has tried the patience of the West. And frequently their own ideological predilections have hampered their grasp of the forces that motivate the policies of nations.

Furthermore, while they agree on broad principles, the leaders of Africa and Asia are divided regarding the content and direction of nonalignment. Among the more radical states, nonalignment has a basic anti-imperialist, and therefore, anti-Western, character. Nkrumah likened nonalignment to the struggle against neo-colonialism. Arguing for independent development, Ghana's former President said: "An external condition for such independent development is neutrality or political nonalignment. . . .And the pre-condition for all this to which lip service is often paid but activity seldom directed, is to develop ideological clarity among the anti-imperialist, anti-colonialist, pro-liberation masses of our continent."[5]

This revolutionary zeal contrasts with the moderate view of President Mba of Gabon: "There is another reason our policy in Gabon consists of seeking cooperation and aid from the developed countries of Europe, America and other continents. We think through such cooperation our country will develop most rapidly. We abstain from taking part in the quarrels which today divide the world into several camps. . . We are Gabonese and Africans. That is enough."[6]

Despite these differences of understanding and interpretation, nonalignment has emerged among the new states as one of the major new forces in international relations. As Professor Peter Worsley has said concerning this new phenomenon, "Conservative and militant alike, reactionary and progressive, socialist and royalist, have shown an extraordinary tendency to adopt similar positions in international affairs."[7]

The Systemic View

Our study of African nonalignment in the pages that follow will be based on a systems or systemic approach. This approach emphasizes the importance of the changing conditioning factors in the international environment, in contrast to the status quo perspective of realism which is preoccupied with conventional views of power in terms of Western technology.[8]

An early critic of the power-factors approach to world politics was Herbert Spiro. He criticized the power-factors view as too static and institutionally oriented. Spiro's study of African nationalism led him to ask how the achievement of independence by the virtually powerless colonies could be explained in a power-ordered world. Moreover, he pointed out that great nuclear powers are greatly inhibited in their relations with less technologically advanced peoples by their fear of nuclear conflict. A systems approach avoids those pitfalls and suggests a more adequate view of the ways new nations form and interact.

Spiro draws from the work of earlier systems analysts such as Easton, but suggests a simpler definition of a political system that covers the smallest to the largest. He says, " . . . A political system can exist wherever people are concerned about common problems and are engaged in cooperation and conflicts in efforts to solve these problems. . . . Individuals or groupings 'units' are involved in politics with one another when they are trying to solve their several problems, together, because each recognizes that it cannot solve its particular problems alone without interaction with the others — even though each may be pursuing different goals."

The existence of a political system is not, Spiro continues, "dependent upon acceptance as legitimate or authoritative of the same goals to compel the other; nor upon the stability over a prolonged period of time of the essential rules governing the process. It depends rather upon the participants' awareness of their participation in the political process."[9]

This political systems concept is especially useful in understanding how new nations are formed out of colonial systems and new international subsystems emerge out of interaction between them for similar goals. The focus is not upon traditional institutions of authority, power, and sovereignty but upon self-identification around new issues and problem-solving through new forms and processes.

The systemic view also related ideology to the conditioning factors in a more meaningful manner. As James Rosenau, in his use of systems analysis, has shown in the development of his "Issue-Areas" concept, conventional views of the state underestimate the role of issues and thereby ideology. As the ideological issue changes, the political system itself changes.[10] Thus, international systems are governed by interrelated changing issues and circumstances. A power-factors approach misses the dynamism of this process because it is balance-of-power oriented and cannot account for the capability of the powerless.

When nonalignment is viewed in terms of the balance of power, its role as an international subsystem is seen as an important but temporary phase in the Cold War.[11] However, the systemic view recognizes an entirely new dimension of an interaction problem-solving political system with a life of its own.

The systemic approach to nonalignment has been utlized partially by Cecil Crabb and to a greater extent by J.W. Burton who have analyzed the phenomenon not in terms of the balance of power but as a prime example of the rapidly changing character of the nation-state system from bipolarity toward multi-configuration systems.[12]

The systemic approach has several unresolved difficulties, such as precise agreement on the proper components of a system, particularly an international subsystem. Even given agreement on such components as authority and integration, it is difficult to agree on how to measure the functions and effectiveness of these components.

The difficulties should not dissuade us from attempting to define these new concepts and to assess their significance, however. The approach has been very rewarding in its insights already but needs to be developed more fully.

Neutrality

Nonalignment should be distinguished from neutralism. Frequently the terms are used interchangeably; but neutrality or neutralism should be used to describe the general historical phenomenon of uncommitted nations in the world system, dominated by the Western powers, before World War II.

Modern nonalignment has antecedents in the old neutralism and even the isolationism of the Western states that developed the neutrality doctrine long recognized in international law. This neutralism included the specific right of nations to remain aloof from war and the rights of her citizens and property to be respected. Sweden and Switzerland have been the longest practitioners of this doctrine in Europe; but numerous nations have employed forms of neutrality, as did the United States in the first phases of both World Wars.

Isolationism is distantly related to modern nonalignment in that it applies to foreign policy in periods of relative peace. But it has been essentially a negative doctrine, as practiced in the United States, and, therefore, is contrary to some of the basic principles of international responsibility incorporated in nonalignment today. Swiss neutralism, by its acceptance of a certain international role as banker, negotiating agent, and sanctuary, is more closely related to modern nonalignment.

Nonalignment gives specific content to the particular policies of the contemporary small powers in the postwar international system.[13] Modern nonalignment, under the impetus of the interdependence and international order, as embodied in the League of Nations and the United Nations, has added the responsibility of all states to prevent conflicts and to help settle them after they have arisen. In a world where every conflict threatens to become a world conflict and where the great powers see their security threatened, all systems come under heavy pressure. Yet, despite this, the new states have demonstrated the significance of their new version of the classic formula.

This new version is frequently referred to by Africans and Asians as "positive neutralism," as a means of contrasting it with the isolationist character of Western neutralism and the old neutrality doctrine. But positive neutralism has also taken on certain militant connotations because of its use by the more revolutionary leaders: — Sukarno, Nasser, and Nkrumah. This distinction will be elaborated upon more fully later.

Origins of Nonalignment

The great-power confrontation since World War II, especially when it escalated to the atomic level and threatened world holocaust, created widespread fear among the emerging peoples that their new expectations would vanish in a sea of flames. This fear, quite logical to those who did not feel threatened directly themselves, led the first successful nationalist leaders, Nehru, Sukarno, Nasser, to seek an alternative to lining up on one side or the other of the nuclear confrontation.

However, the origins of nonalignment do not lie exclusively in the Cold War. The new nationalist leaders of Asia and Africa quickly discovered that they had interests separate from those of the Western world and the communist powers. These interests were not always identified clearly, and frequently were lost in the emotional fervor of anti-imperialism. Nevertheless, they were definite interests that gave a continuing vitality to what might otherwise have evaporated with the failure of early idealistic expectations, the thawing of the Cold War, and the changing structure of great-power relations.

Three basic interests of the new states form the practical ground for nonalignment. They are: 1) self-preservation, 2) cultural and ideological autonomy, and 3) economic growth and modernization.

Fear of involvement in a Third World War if they aligned with one side or the other in the Cold War was the most clearly articulated interest of Asian and African neutral leaders. This fear expressed itself differently, ranging from requests that the great powers withdraw all bases and sever military ties to campaigns at the United Nations for nuclear disarmament and arms control.

Cultural and ideological autonomy was under constant attack during the period of colonialism. The revival of great historical traditions and attempts at the creation of indigenous ideologies have been strong drives of newly independent states in the third world. Their new leaders sought to foster this development by rejecting the values and goals of outside powers and by stressing the formulation of their own. African and Arab socialisms were conceived that encompassed the concept of nonalignment.

Most nationalist leaders opposed what they considered to be economic exploitation by Western colonialism. Therefore, even the more conservative leaders took steps to assure national control of post-independence financial and trading policy. In most cases, complete independence and economic self-determination were clearly impossible for many years to come. However, the belief in this goal became widespread, and a vast array of measures was instituted from exchange control and industrialization to diversified aid and trade programs. The combined effect of these policies within the reality of the new state phenomenon has created the nonaligned subsystem. The essential parts of this type of subsystem are elaborated upon below.

Nonalignment

Nonaligned nations are small powers not subordinate to outside powers who control their own decision-making processes. A. B. Said has a similar definition: "A nonaligned state is one that has no binding military, political, or economic ties to a power center outside its borders. It formulates its foreign and domestic policies, insofar as it can, independently of any outside considerations of allies or bloc leaders." [14]

No nation is completely independent of the influences of other countries, but the essential quality of nonalignment appears to be a high degree of autonomy in decision-making. To some extent, every sovereign nation-state enjoys this status. But sovereignty is a legalistic and rather absolute concept of independence and does not fit the interdependence of nations in the contemporary world. The essence of nonalignment is a conscious and positive nonsubordination and nondominance.

Nonalignment applies primarily to small powers, and in practice these are, for the most part, the new states.[15] The assumption of balance of power analysis as developed by Morgenthau and Walters that small powers are necessarily pulled into the gravitational orbit around one great power must be rejected. Individual and groups of nonaligned nations have a separate self-determining existence within the international system.[16] The basic character of the world is not a balance of power but a complex pattern of power configurations. States fall into two essential categories — great powers and small powers — and the small powers are either aligned or nonaligned. A great power cannot be nonaligned in this concept of the international system because great powers are inherently dominant and create subordinate systems. Small powers are less prone to be dominant, not because they are more equalitarian, but because they are less able to dominate. Therefore, nonalignment is a particularly helpful concept with which to analyze the role of the numerous new nations who, in this era, have strode the world stage so suddenly and boldly.

Components

Some states may conceive of themselves as nonaligned but, in fact, they do not behave according to any definable standards of nonalignment. The status defies exact measurement, and therefore does not easily lend itself to quantitative methods of analysis. Four principal components in various combinations and degrees of influence give shape and character to nonalignment.

The first of these components is diplomatic independence. This is seen most directly in terms of the establishment of an independent diplomatic corps staffed by a country's own nationals with representation in major regions and countries of the world. Recognition of and relations with communist nations, especially the Peoples Republic of China, are particular signs of nonalignment for new states. Other major diplomatic indicators have been voting records and statements at the United Nations. Attendance at third world conferences, which have taken positions on several of the leading issues of the day despite disapproval by the major powers, often has shed further light on a country's stand on nonalignment.

A second major component is military disengagement. Most colonial military forces were associated closely with the defense systems of the mother countries. As a consequence of independence, foreign troops have been withdrawn, foreign officers phased out, bases closed, and new sources of military training and supply employed.

Economic diversification is the third component. The colonial single-crop type of economy, virtually dependent upon the mother country, is transformed slowly by diversified development and new trade and aid patterns. These are extended to include all the major markets and sources of supply and aid in the world, including the communist powers.

The fourth component is ideological and cultural self-identification. Western cultural assimilation is rejected in favor of the cultivation of national heritage and accomplishment. Indigenous interpretation of social change and revolutionary goals is projected, as demonstrated in Arab or African socialism.

Subsystems

The international system includes various types of subsystems. The essential characteristics of *all* subsystems can be compressed into two functions: 1) an identifiable pattern of attempted interstate problem-solving among three or more participants; 2) some evidence of social and economic integration.

The first characteristic may not necessarily be institutionalized, though in the more developed forms it is. The second characteristic of integration can be measured over a period of time and analyzed in terms of intensity and degree. Obviously, the patterns of subsystems vary widely from the less formalized to the highly developed. This field has been intensively analyzed.[17]

A nonalignment subsystem is a group of three or more nonaligned states that form a functioning political system based on 1) political cultural identity, 2) problem-solving, 3) self-policing characteristics, 4) some economic and social integration, and 5) non-subordination to an external power.

Identity here means a political culture consciousness and behavior based on a distinguishable nexus of basic values, attitudes, and assumptions. In the international system, these are very broad, distinguishing the North American from the South American, the European from the Arab, and the African from the Asian. This identity is usually symbolized by a political authority.

Professor I. William Zartman has described the functional characteristics of a subsystem as "problem-solving and self-maintenance."[18] Problem-solving includes all the basic problems of economic development and integration of regions. Because a subsystem can be a very primitive political organism, significant economic integration may be only beginning or may be quite advanced. The major problem-solving concern of such a system is to coordinate the external policies of its members.

The function of self-maintenance refers to the policing and arbitration of disputes among members and between the nonaligned system and external powers. A nonaligned system could establish a collective defense system, but none has done this yet. Generally they perform very limited functions in settling internal disputes and preventing intervention by the outside world.

A nonaligned subsystem is autonomous because its constituent parts are not subordinate to any power grouping. It usually establishes its identity and legitimizes its authority by creating a formal organization, as, in the case of Africa, the Organization of African Unity (OAU).

Non-subordination does not mean that external powers have no influence within the nonaligned system. Great powers have influence in a variety of forms. The essential quality is not sovereignty, which is a meaningless term from a political systems view. External assistance may be sought in surmounting problems, but the subsystem organizes resistance to external control over the problem-solving process.

Obviously, the point at which a subsystem passes from subordination to self-control is not precise. The forces within a developing nonaligned subsystem press away from external power dominance and toward autonomous problem-solving and interaction with the international system.[19] Rival subsystems, reflecting different policies or regional interests within a given area, may exist within an overall nonaligned system. This rivalry may well threaten the identity of the system. Such groupings may be organized formally in an international institution or informally as caucus groups.

Conclusion

The study of any nonaligned subsystem raises a great many significant questions for the theory and practice of international relations. First, it questions the bipolar view of the world still held by many analysts. Even those who limit this bipolarism to nuclear powers must face the issue of the nuclear stalemate and the consequent diffusion of power to other factors.

As nonalignment is systemic, its special role within the system has to be defined. Moreover, nonalignment takes different forms. Minimal nonalignment is best determined not so much in terms of theory as in behavior. We need to identify the more effective forms of nonalignment.

We must be explicit about the major criteria for nonalignment and the function of subsystems in international relations. The term multipolar does not really reflect the power structure of a world where new nonaligned systems have emerged. They do not constitute major power blocs themselves nor are they directly attached to major powers. Therefore, new terminology and theory is required for a plural world system with many concentric circles of power configuration.

International systems theory has opened up new ways of thinking about and understanding the operations of the changing world system. A systemic view of political systems breaks through the formal barriers of sovereignty and power to a new understanding of the functional roles of states in servicing the aspirations of their citizens.

The concept of a nonaligned subsystem is highly applicable to the African continent where numerous new states have suddenly sprung up. In assessing the character and growth of this subsystem, we hope to gain some insights into the practical problems of the new African states as well as to establish theoretical concepts useful in the analysis of new states in general and the international system as a whole.

A subsystem can fragment and collapse or strengthen and extend itself to its logical geographic limits. All these possibilities are present in Africa. A study of nonalignment should, therefore, raise all the relevant questions about the capacity of the system to meet the demands placed upon it or about its tendency to disintegrate under internal strains and external pressures.

Thus in the study of any nonaligned subsystem, we must consider first its origins and component parts. Secondly, we must look at its functioning problems and changing patterns. Finally, we must reach some conclusions about its weaknesses and strengths and overall role within the international system.

2

The Racial and Colonial Origins of African Nonalignment

Africa has many more nonaligned nations than does any other continent. Therefore, Africa must have special environmental and historical conditions especially conducive to the growth of this particular national stance. Development of a substantial nonalignment system may rank in history among Africa's most significant contributions to the world.

At the 1955 Bandung Conference in Indonesia, Africa and Asia enunciated the famous ten principles, including "respect for the sovereignty and territorial integrity of all nations; abstention from intervention or interference in the internal affairs of another country; abstention from the use of arrangements of collective defense to serve the particular interests of any of the big powers; abstention by any country from exerting pressures on other countries; and settlement of all international disputes by peaceful means . . . ."[1]

The Conference was significant, not because it stated something new, but because of the presence of so many countries from the emerging nations who found, at least for the moment, an elusive unity that was later referred to as "the Bandung spirit."

Only five African states participated in the Conference: The Gold Coast, Liberia, Ethiopia, Egypt, and Libya. But, after 1955, the number of African states emerging on the world scene increased rapidly and the locus of international conferences of nonaligned nations shifted to Africa and the Middle East. The All-African Peoples Organization met in Accra in 1958, in Tunis in 1960, and in Cairo in 1961. These early conferences found an identity of interest and a common language for expressing their attempts to carve out a new role in world affairs that launched, but could not long sustain, the cooperation of all the rapidly emerging African states. Later, at Belgrade, Cairo, and Algiers, a series of conferences expressed the attempts of Afro-Asian nations to unite on common principles.

Although the terms "Afro-Asian bloc" and "nonalignment alliance" have been used often to describe the actions of these nations, no true bloc, but rather a very transitory cooperation on broad principles, was established among them. However, if the African states are considered by themselves, a far clearer pattern of nonalignment behavior emerges. It is discernible, not only at the meetings of the independent African states from 1958-1963, but also at the United Nations, that certain groupings characterized the voting and policy positions of the new African states from the start.[2] This nonalignment stance was far from monolithic, with substantial differences in policy and formal and informal rival groups. Nevertheless, the distinctive outlines of a nonalignment system had emerged in the foreign policies of African states by 1960.

Origins and Types of African Nonalignment: The Moral View

Much of the argument for nonalignment has been couched in moral terms. This view has projected a strong Utopian notion that at last the world had evolved a number of nation-states who would be freed from the compromising, power-hungry pursuit of national ambitions that led to conflict in international relations for so long. As Margaret Legum put it, this view saw Africa as "opting out of power politics,"[3] and would, through nonalignment, be able to approach with clean hands the age-old problems of peace-making, thereby providing new hope for peace in the world.

African nonalignment policies may approach these problems from new perspectives, but they do not stem from a new morality that has arisen suddenly among Afro-Asian nations. Small powers are less restricted by the dilemmas of power and responsibility characteristic of great powers. They think they are better able to project policies based on moral considerations rather than on the self-interest and compromises that restrict great powers. The attitude among new nations toward what they regard as the corruption and decadence of the West lends weight to this view. But attractive as this view of the origins of nonalignment may be to Afro-Asians, it reflects a very simple view of the behavior of nations. It does not interpret realistically the moral dilemmas of power at all levels, and has not been borne out by experience. Nevertheless, the motivating force of a new morality in non-Western ideologies is very powerful. The extent of the influence of the sense of self-righteousness against Western "decadence" among African intellectuals is reflected in the popularity of the Algerian revolutionary Franz Fanon's *The Wretched of the Earth.*

Anti-Colonial Racial Identity

The anti-colonialism and equalitarianism of African nationalism have been major sources of nonalignment. The heritage of slavery and colonial exploitation that all African nationalists share alienates them from continued dependency upon the Western world. Some states, particularly the French-speaking ones, were less anxious than others to separate themselves from the mother power, but even they harbored bitter memories of colonial wars and indignities of white rule strong enough to maintain the momentum toward separation from metropolitan dominance.

As a result of their subjection by the white man, Africans have a highly developed sense of race consciousness. This consciousness is related closely to culture but reinforces their sense of racial identity. This color consciousness goes far back into the historical relationship of races in Africa; but the establishment of a dominant-subordinate relationship undoubtedly intensified it. Color, as a ready means of identity, performed the role of distinguishing between the rulers and the ruled under slavery and colonialism. Thus, in reaction to European racism, the African emerged from colonialism with, in some instances, a counter-racism, and, in others, a keen group identity built upon race consciousness.

This sense of racial as well as cultural identity strengthened African aspirations to separate their political forms from Europe. European assimilation attempts failed to convince the revolutionary leaders in the former African colonies that they should become black Frenchmen or Englishmen. They wanted to find their own African personality. Vague as was their awareness of it, nevertheless they felt committed to the new African personality because they could not identify with a European political culture that had subjected them to the indignities of racial prejudice.

Pan-Africanism

Pan-Africanism arose out of these same racial and ethnic feelings. It attempted to extend these ideas on a continental basis across the barriers of colonial and new state systems. In contrast to Asian nationalism, which was split into contending cultural groups, African nationalism, in its earliest stages, had a strong pan-nationalist drive that superficially suppressed ethnic differences.

Essentially, Pan-Africanism was a projection of the community of blackness. For a time, its appeal transcended all the differences of language and culture that post-independent Africa found so divisive. The more Utopian early African thinkers and leaders rallied substantial support to the ideal of the unity of the African continent as a means of maximizing strength and independence. Though disillusionment over the prospects for unity followed, the basic yearning for self-identification as Africans remained. This contributed significantly to the idea that Africa had separate interests from the outside world.

Assimilation

The more realistic African leaders have viewed nonalignment as an opportunity to detach themselves more fully from great power domination and assimilation. Emperor Haile Selassie, speaking of the great importance of the United Nations in preserving African independence, said, "For us, the small, the weak, the underdeveloped, there is nowhere else to go. If we turn to one of the major power groups, we risk engorgement, that gradual process of assimilation which destroys identity and personality."[4]

The Cold War

All these factors were overshadowed for a time by the impact of the Cold War. When most Asian states achieved independence, the Cold War was not underway fully, in contrast to the Korean and Hungarian crises that mark the African era of emergence of the 1950's. Asian nonalignment was conceived within the widespread spirit of international cooperation in the early postwar years. The United Nations had been established, and collective security was regarded widely as a hopeful basis for peace. Asian nonalignment, as proposed by Prime Minister Nehru, was designed primarily for small-power mediation in world politics. When the Cold War undermined the security provided by United Nations membership, the motive for neutralism intensified. Yet, some Asian powers, such as Pakistan, Iran, and the Philippines, had already made a commitment to the West and nonalignment never was accepted as broadly in Asia as in Africa.

African states came into the world during the height of the Cold War. They were confronted with a harsh reality. To associate closely with one or the other side meant to be involved in a conflict which appeared to be on the brink of spilling over into hot war. Therefore, almost all new African states felt in varying degrees that their own security and development could be assured best outside the framework of the Cold War. Only Liberia and Ethiopia made any significant commitment to the West. A realistic African political observer, Professor Ali Mazrui, frequently has stressed the importance of the Cold War in bringing about African nonalignment. In discussing the significance of nonalignment at the United Nations, he was skeptical of its contribution to peace between the great powers but stressed the importance of the Cold War to the capacity of the African states to take independent positions. He said, "It is not a case of nonalignment making peace possible, it is more a case of the fear of war making nonalignment possible."[5] In another connection he argued that it was really to the advantage of the African states to keep the Cold War going, although he believed that fortunately they are not that self-interested.[6]

The Cold War has had both an idealistic and a realistic influence on the development of African nonalignment. Several African leaders, notably Nkrumah, Nasser, and Nyerere, have argued that the small African states can play a key role in helping keep the peace of the world. This is why they have stressed the words, "positive neutralism." They have felt committed positively to finding compromise solutions to great-power confrontations in Berlin, Cuba, and Vietnam, as well as the crises on the African continent, such as Suez and the Congo.

Beyond the Cold War

With the nature of the Cold War changing, the question arises: Will this mean a diminishing force behind nonalignment? In the case of India, particularly since the Sino-Indian border war, the voices advocating a policy of nonalignment have been much weaker. In Africa, a similar disillusionment does not appear to have taken place for several reasons.

No major communist or Western power exists on the Continent of Africa. Moreover, Africa is not threatened with direct invasion by any communist power. The Sino-Soviet split has increased suspicion regarding the ultimate intentions of the communist powers because the rival communist groups resort to fantastic intrigue in seeking influence with the new African states and "liberation" movements. Since the 1964 Congo crisis, Western powers have been more circumspect concerning intervention.

The French departure from NATO has made the French-speaking states less inclined to associate closely with the United States as the leader of the Western bloc. This view is encouraged by France, whose policy is to draw Africa as close as possible to the European Common Market.

Nonalignment in Africa does not depend upon the Cold War, but transcends it. The urge for development which pits the poor against the rich derives from much more fundamental differences than the ideological disputes of the Cold War. It is a North-South confrontation in which the poor African nations attempt to develop themselves with the assistance of the more developed nations. This is difficult but their dignity and their aspirations demand it. Deeply sensitive to what they regard as assimilationist tendencies of great powers, East and West, whom, they suspect, do not dole out economic aid for purely philanthropic reasons, weak small powers seek a more complete independence through nonalignment.

Some new states are more realistic than others about the continuing degree to which their development programs must continue to depend on the support of the Western powers. Yet all feel, to some degree, that they can benefit from the diversification of their old aid and trade patterns. Therefore, new relations have opened up, beyond their former metropolitan powers, with the United States, the Soviet Union, and China.

Frequently, they use the rival interests of these great powers to obtain greater assistance. During the height of the Cold War, the ideological rivalry provided a convenient pressure point. This Cold War may be continuing in new forms and may be far from over. However, even without a Cold War the great powers would compete for influence and trade with the emerging nations. The reaction to this rivalry by the disadvantaged African nations, with a keen eye to their own best interests of development, constitutes the primary moving force behind nonalignment in Africa today.

Nonalignment in Africa is not just an ideological game or an attempt to moralize about world problems. It is grounded in the interests and necessities of economic prosperity and modernization, as realistic as the policies of older states. This does not mean that all the diversified aid programs, particularly with the communist states, have been purely business propositions or even wise undertakings contributing to development. Obviously, many of them have not been, as Ghana under Nkrumah demonstrated so well. The question of effectiveness will be discussed later. Here we are concerned with the motivations of the African states in undertaking this kind of activity, as noted by Margaret Legum: "It was the result of cool calculation of the advantages and disadvantages, political, economic and psychological, of aligning with one of the major blocs, as compared with those of nonalignment."[7]

The conviction is spreading, not only in Africa but throughout the underdeveloped world, that the rich nations of the world are not devoted genuinely to improving the plight of the impoverished majority. According to this conviction, the rich fear the revolutions of have-nots and a possible alliance of the poor with Communist China, but relish their rising standards of living more and are not interested in fundamental changes in the status quo. They say the gospel of the status quo is, "To the rich it will be given, and from the poor it will be withheld."

The West may feel that this distorts our motives and misinterprets what is actually happening. Yet, the underprivileged are not inclined to blame themselves if the bright new world fails to arrive. As Ronald Segal observed in *The Race War*: "The poor themselves inevitably see the collaboration of the rich as a 'ganging up against' alliance to preserve and indeed increase the privileges of the past."[8] Given this view of the world, it is not surprising that the new nations of Africa resist what they feel are assimilationist pressures by the great powers and attempt to develop independent patterns of economic growth. They intend to create economic systems relevant to the diverse needs of their own peoples, and these may, at points, conflict with the economic interests of Europe, the United States, or the Soviet Union.

Communist China is attractive to some of the developing African states because they feel that the Chinese are neither developed exploiters nor underdeveloped exploited. In time, they may discover as have nations of Southeast Asia, that this is not entirely the case. However, the non-Western, non-white character of the Chinese Peoples Republic gives it at least a different image to those for whom the Cold War is secondary to their intense aspiration for economic progress.

External Subversion

The fear of internal strife stirred by rival neo-colonial influences has also been a major concern of Africa's leaders. African single-party and military systems are not noted for their tolerance of opposition. In many ways these authoritarian political forms are reactions to the internal instability of the new states. A number of African heads of state have been virtually paranoic over the intervention of great-power political influences in their internal affairs. Certainly, there have been grounds for this as the classic Congo crisis of 1960 illustrated. Not all the coups d'etat are attributable to foreign influence, and there has been a great deal of starting at shadows. Nevertheless, the political atmosphere of most new African states has become charged with the suspicion of possible foreign influence.

This fear of outside intervention is a natural part of the emergence of the small, weak states. The attempt to insulate internal politics from external intervention by maintaining a position of nonalignment has become a major concern that will continue as long as African governments are so insecure that a student or army rebellion can overthrow them.

The African Personality

Finally, the quest of the African for dignity and personality must be noted. Frequently, this has been couched in terms of an attempt to build an African socialism independent of East and West. Under Cold War pressures, Africans have felt compelled to emphasize their political independence and intellectual freedom. Regardless of the Cold War, Africans would have asserted their unique traditions and political perspectives. Colonialism, with its racist arrogance, has created a resurgence of African pride in their past, and stimulated an effort by African intellectuals to achieve a synthesis of Western values with African communalism.

In the African concepts of personality and Negritude, a ground of being and identity is formulating. The political culture implied in these concepts provides a firm foundation for nonalignment. African pride in its uniqueness, as much as fear of neo-colonialism, has created the motivation to be nonaligned. While this nonalignment takes various forms in response to what the African believes are the requisites of his freedom, the basic world view of Africanism must be nonaligned to retain its own essential character. Like most cultural concepts, this is abstract and poetic. No one has expressed these ideas more completely than the Senegalese poet, politician, and philosopher, Leopold Senghor:

In the struggle of the blocs, the conflict of ideologies, the profusion of scientific discoveries and technical inventions, we must keep a cool head and an attentive heart. Once again we must assimilate, not be assimilated. More exactly, it is a question of remaining deeply rooted in our Negritude. [9]

Nonalignment at this point becomes less realistic and self-interested, and evolves into idealistic expressions of freedom and self-realization. This is one reason African political leaders are devoted so intensely to the liberation of all of Africa. They see in the continuation of racial and colonial forms of subjection a compromise of their own freedom. South African racism symbolizes the weakness and slavery of Africa's early contact with the Western world. Nonalignment thus becomes a commitment to utilize every available African resource to purge Africans of this memory of their bondage to the white man. They would like to liberate Africa themselves, yet are terribly frustrated by their lack of power to accomplish it alone. Therefore, they turn to the West and the East and appeal to the sentiments of both for assistance.

The most realistic African leaders realize that they cannot defeat white supremacy in Southern Africa without the cooperation of the United States and Great Britain, but they know that this support will stop short of force, and, therefore, they must get arms from the communist world. In doing this, they walk a very perilous tightrope for they cannot take arms from the Communists to the point where they endanger their nonaligned status and alienate the West. On the other hand, they must be revolutionary enough to get the Communist arms they need to defeat the Portuguese, Rhodesians, and South Africans. There are many dilemmas and dangers.

Nonalignment as a basic African position in world affairs is a major response by Africans to the kind of world conditions from which they emerged. It rests on more than ideology and has roots in the existential nature of the new states themselves.

The nonalignment subsystem in Africa has developed its own character. However, this international subsystem contains a number of variations in policy, style, and tactics. These variations arise from the differing conditions of development and viewpoints of leaders. These distinctions must be brought out in assessing the nature of African nonalignment, its strengths and weaknesses.

No two African states follow identical nonalignment policies. Thomas Hovet in his studies found Ghana (under Nkrumah), Guinea, and Mali had only a five percent variation in their votes on key issues at the United Nations. However, this cohesion is quite unusual and other African groupings were considerably divided on major issues, though they tend to fall into patterns.[10]

The major distinguishing sources of African foreign policies originate in the extent of their modernization, the character of their colonial origins, their cultural heritage, and the ideologies of their leaders. Variations in the nonalignment of African states may be traced to each of these variables. Algeria is oriented to the Arab world. Tunisia is more highly Westernized. Ghana (under Nkrumah) and Guinea accepted Marxist revolutionary tenets not shared by many others. Mutual suspicion, as well as rival interests, have characterized the relations of French- and British-speaking African nations.

In terms of the components of nonalignment discussed in Chapter 1 (ideology, economics, military ties, and diplomacy), African states vary substantially in theory and practice. No patterns are identical. Each state combines these components differently. Some, like Senegal and Nigeria, emphasize economic concerns; others give primacy to ideological or diplomatic interests, as during the Nkrumah decade in Ghana.

Despite these dissimilarities, the nonaligned African states fall into two basic ideological types. Ideology is the central organizing factor influencing all the others. It should be seen in Africa not as a consistent modern doctrine of the state but as a political perspective of basic values and goals derived from indigenous culture as much as from universal theories of society.

James Coleman and Carl Rosberg, in their comparative study of national integration and African political parties, made this kind of primary distinction among African political systems by utilizing the categories of "central revolutionary" and "plural pragmatic" in distinguishing methods of organization and political ideology.[11] Since foreign policy is related closely to internal politics, this kind of distinction is useful in analyzing nonalignment policies. Coleman and Rosberg point out that in the centralized revolutionary forms of African governments "positive neutralism" characterizes the ideology of foreign policy, whereas in the plural pragmatic systems a more moderate form of nonalignment is typical.[12] The major discernible variable is the highly specific ideological doctrine of the revolutionary states.

One group of African states, then, has developed what can be called radical nonalignment. Such states as Ghana, Guinea, Mali, Algeria, Egypt, Congo-Brazzaville, and Tanzania have at various points in their brief histories manifested characteristics of alienation and innovation typical of this kind of nonalignment. In African terminology, positive neutralism is used most frequently to describe this approach.

The Radicals

The ideology of radical nonalignment is influenced strongly by Marxism, though the leadership is careful to draw distinctions between European communist brands and African Marxism. As Sékou Touré expressed it, "It is evident that certain Marxist concepts suit African conditions but it is no less evident that Africa will have to find its own revolutionary principles."[13] Yet, despite this Africanization of socialism, many strong influences from Marxist doctrine create rigid categories of thought, such as the necessity to nationalize private industries and the imperialistic tendencies of capitalism over and against the equalitarianism of socialism.

Neo-colonialism is a major concept of the Afro-Marxists who are inclined to interpret the motives of the Western powers in this context. The effect of this has been to intensify fear of Western assimilation and to give an anti-Western bias to many of the assessments of international conflict by the Afro-Marxists. At times of international crisis, such as the Stanleyville Drop in 1964, neo-colonialism has blended the position of the revolutionary Africans with that of the communist powers and has led to widespread misconceptions in the Western world that this form of nonalignment was nothing more than a camp-follower of the communist world. However, a careful assessment of all relevant factors leads to a different conclusion.

Another aspect of this system is ideological conformity leading to political regimentation and the limitation of alternative sources of information and opinion. Therefore, a party line frequently emerges and is used by those in power to enforce conformity through the highly centralized political apparatus. In this way, a line on external issues often becomes an internal political weapon of centralized control. Because of the lack of criticism and alternative information, such a system typically is characterized by doctrinairism and paranoia.

The economic policies of the "positive neutralists" include major attempts to open trade and aid arrangements with the communist world. On certain occasions, this was necessitated by the sudden termination of Western economic relations, as with Guinea in 1958. In theory, nonalignment requires these new relationships in order to eliminate total economic dependency on the Western world. The positive neutralists regard this as especially important, for they fear the insidious consequences of neo-colonialism from the Western world far more than they do from the East.

The military strategies of the members of this group are very similar. They permit no bases of great powers or alliance with the giants. However, arms supply and training is diversified. Some of them, such as Algeria and Egypt, depend on communist sources of support much more than other nonaligned states have felt necessary. Again, fear of neo-colonialism as well as alienation from the West in a military struggle, as in Algeria, has led to this extent of diversification.

Extensive diplomatic ties with the communist world is the third major characteristic of the radical camp. They relish and even flaunt their recognition of Communist China as a symbol of their independence and nonalignment. They have had few reservations about cultural and informational exchange. As a consequence, while they have restricted Western sources of information, frequently these countries have been flooded with the propaganda of communist cultural missions. Student and auxiliary party exchange groups and study missions travel back and forth constantly. However, in recent years this kind of activity has been limited because of its unproductivity and dangerous political consequences. More than once, the radical leaders have discovered that their new friends in the communist world support subversive groups in their countries while pledging solidarity publicly.

Pragmatists

The second major group of nonaligned African states can be called the pragmatists. While they share many aspirations and policies with the revolution-aries, they are far less ideologically motivated and unified. Their policies are governed by the practical and, they would say realistic limitations of their underdevelopment and colonial inheritance.

Often the pragmatists describe their ideology as "African socialism." However, usually Marxist conceptions such as neo-colonialism are not dominant. Neo-colonialism is considered a slogan more than a reality and less a threat to independence than the continuance of underdevelopment and poverty. Their socialism draws more on the Western democratic socialist practices of England and Scandinavia. The idea of the good society and its moral foundation as found in the thought of both Mboya and Nyerere shows the Fabian influence clearly.[14]

For the pragmatists their economic ties with the Western world are primary. This dependence will diminish, they feel, as they develop. But, for the present, they doubt that they would benefit from substantial diversification. Most of them regard association with the European Common Market as necessary, although the Commonwealth of Nations members are far less active than the French-speaking states in the EEC.

At times, the pragmatists have entered some limited military agreements in addition to purchasing arms. Nigeria had a defense agreement with Great Britain until 1962. Several French-speaking states have maintained French bases in their territories. British aircraft carriers cruise off the African coasts. The trend, however, is away from direct ties of this nature among this group of the nonaligned. At times of crisis, actions counter to this trend, such as calling in French or British troops to put down an insurrectionary movement, have been taken. But they have been quickly withdrawn and an African force substituted, as in Tanzania in 1964.

Nonaligned diplomacy involves dealing with the communist world. The pragmatists limit these contacts to those communist states from whom they feel they can benefit most directly. In many cases, this does not include Communist China, while relations are maintained with Taiwan.

Conclusions on Origins and Nature

African nonalignment is as much the product of the colonial and under-developed background of national emergence as of the Cold War. The Cold War gave impetus to the radical brand of nonalignment. On the other hand, the pragmatic approach to nonalignment reflects the underlying reality of under-development that effects the emergence of colonial states into the world political system.

The existence in Asia and particularly in Latin America of many under-developed nations which are not nonaligned does not alter this conclusion. The direct experience of colonialism is essential to the development of nonalignment. The anti-imperialist spirit and counter-racist psychology of emergence from colonialism create the setting for alignment.

Therefore, the transformation of the Cold War by the American-Russian detente and the Sino-Soviet split has not reduced significantly the impetus that nonalignment has in Africa. This contrasts with Asia where China has a great power sphere of influence directly bordering a number of nonaligned states, such as India and Burma.

In a recent study of the Third World, J. D. B. Miller concluded, "It is likely that nonalignment will survive in something like the same way as monarchy survives in Britain; as a frequently useful but not essential aspect of policy, which would be difficult to dispose of but is not permitted to stand in the way of necessary action when a government is convinced that action must be taken."[15]

This interpretation fails to make the essential distinction between the radical and the moderate forms of nonalignment. Often, the more revolutionary policies of African governments have sacrificed immediate benefits to an ideological commitment.

The type of nonalignment likely to prevail in Africa is influenced, of course, by the intensity of the Cold War. Radical nonalignment has suffered substantial setbacks with the fall of Ben Bella, the departure of Nkrumah, and the rise of several new military governments that are inclined toward moderation in foreign relations. The Russians have not responded to the appeal of revolutionary leaders like Nkrumah for help when they have encountered difficulties, because they are less anxious than they have been to preserve this type of African government. The flirtations of Nkrumah and Ben Bella with the Chinese probably did a lot of damage in Moscow, but even more important, the Sino-Soviet split divided the left wing in these revolutionary countries. This weakened them in their struggles with the pro-Western moderates and military, thereby laying the basis for coups from the right.

In addition, the pragmatists have demonstrated a slightly better capacity to handle the difficult problems of development. Their economic failures affected the foreign aid positions of Nkrumah and Touré. Nyerere, in Tanzania, has shown greater responsibility and efficiency. Yet, his insistence on nonalignment has cost him dearly with West Germans and, increasingly, with the United States.[a]

Pragmatic nonalignment appears to the West to be more legitimate. While the West has not undermined the position of the revolutionary nonaligned deliberately, the revolutionaries have increasingly alienated Western governments, causing them to withhold assistance and, in some cases, to lend immediate support to more moderate elements able to replace the revolutionaries.

With the decline of revolutionary posturing over nonalignment, a more receptive and constructive atmosphere for growth is being created. Beneath the surface conflicts, a great deal of constructive planning, consulting, and integrating has been taking place. The consensus developing among African professional diplomats and experts is strengthening nonalignment.

The nonalignment subsystem appears to encompass the behavior of both the pragmatic and the radical African states. The Africans have created an autonomous political culture out of traditional beliefs and modern methods, best identified as the African Personality or Negritude. A problem-solving system, both formal and informal, has been established for the African Continent. As imperfect as the arbitration and mediation attempts have been, they have functioned. As subsequent chapters demonstrate, economic and social institutions of integration have been created among African states. In addition, this subsystem attempts to police itself and it is generally not subordinate to an external power. These are the major criteria of an international subsystem as observed in Chapter 1. The imperfections of a system are evidence of its weakness rather than its non-existence. They may also be indications of growth or decay. The ways in which this system is subject to challenge and the effectiveness of the African response are considered in subsequent chapters.

[a]The return of American aid to Ghana after the overthrow of Nkrumah is a clear-cut example of such preferential treatment.

3

Regional Rivalries and Caucuses Within the African Subsystem

On no other continent has the aspiration for unity been so intensely shared by as wide a spectrum of leaders as in Africa. Pan-Africanism was a cardinal article of faith of the revolutionary nationalists who, during World War II, plotted the creation of new nations. The roots of the idea go back into the history of the struggle of the black peoples in the New World in this century. H. Sylvester Williams, George Padmore and W. E. B. Du Bois chronicled the contributions of the West Indians to the development of "Pan-Negroism."[1] Of equal importance within the Franco-African tradition was the poet Aimé Césaire from Martinique.

The necessity and reality of the unity of the black-skinned and exploited peoples against the great colonizing powers was the formative idea they posited. As W. E. B. Du Bois predicted at the beginning of this century, "The problem of the twentieth century will be the problem of the color line." This color line has clearly both united and divided Africa.

George Padmore and his disciple, Kwame Nkrumah, were inspired by this theme and adapted it directly to Africa. Padmore's influence was largely limited to the period of the nationalist struggle, and was best exemplified in his book, *Pan-Africanism or Communism*. As head of the first independent black African state, Nkrumah called for an all-African political union to consolidate freedom on the African continent, and to resist neo-colonialism. At first, this appeal was warmly embraced in principle by all nationalist African leaders. Later, major differences arose over how to achieve this unity and what its content should be.

The close relationship between Pan-African aspirations and the origins of the African nonalignment subsystem have been noted already. The early intensity of the Pan-African spirit gave hope to African leaders that a united Africa could be a major part of a third force in the world. This third force was to help Africa obtain her needs for development and remove much of the war-producing rivalry of the great powers. If, indeed, such unity could be achieved, a nonaligned African system could mediate global conflicts and bargain vigorously for aid and greater autonomy.

However, Pan-Africanism splintered into rival camps and African unity became an unrealized dream. The effect of this upon the nonaligned subsystem has been substantial but not fatal. Few African leaders admit publicly their frustrations over the lack of cooperative policy among African states. Structures have been created like the OAU, the East Africa Common Services Organization, and OCAM, but they are largely hulks without cargo, left on the sand bars of Africa by the tides of hope that launched them and then receded. Yet, tides ebb and flow and they may float again.

One reaction to this collapse of early expectations of Pan-Africanism has been to conclude that nationalism and tribalism have taken over completely. The OAU and even regional agencies of unity are discounted as romantic illusions and the existence of any significant distinctive pan-national political system in Africa is denied.[2]

This denial is too extreme. It grows not only from disillusionment but also from a legalistic and constitutional view of political systems that emphasizes traditional concepts of power. The functional view of the nature of political systems provides a different perspective. This view assesses the effectiveness of political systems in terms of the concepts of the subsystem, i.e., identity, problem-solving, self-policing, economic and social integration, and autonomy (see Chapter 1).

Evaluation of the Pan-African movements in these terms produces conclusions that differ from much of the conventional wisdom. Two main patterns in Pan-Africanism fit the subsystem concept. These tend to weave together in a complex manner. The idea of one all-embracing union of African states on a geographic continental basis is one pattern. The other is regional-functional and the limited integration of closely related African states.

The regional pattern came first as a result of organizational efforts of the first African states to obtain independence. The goal of an all-encompassing union was finally achieved under the OAU in 1963. Since then, as a result of the rivalries and failures of the OAU, the regional pattern has returned in various guises — as caucuses of certain states and as officially established entities in others.

Conflicts exist between the regional systems and the overall African system centered in the OAU and among the regional systems. Nevertheless, taken together they form what has been called here the African subsystem.

Patterns of Rivalry

Patterns of regional Pan-African cooperation have emerged among African states, as the basic coordinating units of transnational activity. Yet, the significance of these patterns and the reason for their formation is a subject of considerable controversy. Some have come and gone; others have had a more durable existence.

The most important cohesive factor has been the link with a common metropolitan power. In most cases, this has been derived from a shared colonial heritage. Despite all the bitterness of the anti-colonial struggle, those states that were linked together by their subjection to England or France find that they continue to have a great affinity in independence. The reason is that the colonial system built interlocking economic and services networks, as well as cultural perspective, that provide a solid basis for external policy. Thus, since 1960 the French-speaking states of former French West and Equatorial Africa have consistently formed various regional associations, from the Union of Africa and Malagasy (UAM) to the most recent OCAM. All of these have been closely related to France.

The former British colonies of East and Central Africa also have explored various forms of cooperation, from PAFMECA to the East African Common Services Organization. Their membership in the Commonwealth of Nations has symbolized their acceptance of close links with Great Britain.

The French regional groupings have been the largest and most consistent. From time to time they have been joined to a limited extent by others with different origins, such as Liberia and Rwanda. Former British territories have not had the same consistency of unity, as the early rivalry of Ghana and Nigeria demonstrated. And the harmony among Francophone states has often been broken by sharp conflicts. The hostility between Touré and Houphouet-Boigny has been one of the sharpest dividing points.

This colonial basis of cooperation has been counteracted by a number of other formative influences. Not least among these is culture. Arab and Islamic Africa have a special cohesion of their own. This is not always consistent, as the periodic disaffection of Tunisia has shown, but the cohesion of Egypt, Algeria, Mali, and to some extent, the Sudan, has been remarkably high, despite their well-known differences. Between Arabs of the Middle East (UAR) and the Maghreb Arabs there is sufficient mutuality to produce a high degree of cooperation. Morocco, Algeria, and the Sudan are members of the Arab League whose leaders on the whole take religion and culture seriously.

These sources of interest and perspective in addition to their conflict with Israel are productive of a common world view, if not common internal policies. Thus, a French-speaking Arab state like Algeria will have a different perspective from a former French colony in "Afrique Noire."

Culture is another primary source of cohesion in a group of middle African Bantu states. This group, consisting of Uganda, Tanzania, Nigeria, Ghana, Guinea, and Chad, cuts across the usual colonial and ideological lines of unity to form a wider grouping of Bantu states. In voting at the United Nations and in debates at the OAU they show a high degree of cohesion. However, this bond is the most tenuous of all integrative factors, as it is linked to traditional, pre-European cultural patterns. The Bantu culture is very diffuse in comparison to the Arab bonds of North Africa.[3] Its ideological exponents are the proponents of the concept of Negritude, like Senghor, and the major lines of demarcation have been made by cultural anthropologists such as Melville Herskovits and Evans Pritchard.

These factors conducive to cooperation have a way of reinforcing themselves.

Ideology has been noted earlier as a major integrative, as well as divisive, factor. When revolutionary ideology is combined with a strong cultural unity, high cohesion results, as in the cases of the UAR, Algeria, and Mali. A similar phenomenon explains the high cohesion of the former French territories of the Entente — the Ivory Coast, Dahomey, Upper Volta, and Niger.

In contrast to this, very little has come of formal association agreements among African states such as the Union of African States of Ghana, Guinea, and Mali. Much of the reason lies in the attempt to stretch ideological perspectives over a number of major economic, historical, and cultural differences. Ideological affinity does not seem to be enough to achieve a high level of integration of foreign policies of the type projected in the Union of African States. Of great importance is the direction of economic integration among the African states, the trade and aid programs, and the nature of the domestic economic development effort.

So far very few African states have been able to develop new and meaningful patterns of economic integration. However, certain attempts have been made which have given significant impetus to cohesive policies. The outstanding case is Tanzania, a merger of Tanganyika and Zanzibar. On a regional level, the East African Common Services Organization attempts to integrate more fully the economies of Kenya, Tanzania and Uganda. Until recently, the trend has been toward less rather than more cooperation. The failure of East Africa's political leaders to give any substance to their mutual declarations of intention to form an East African Federation is a classic example of the futility in this field. Yet, a revived interest has been shown in functional cooperation through the adoption of the Common Market concepts of the East African Common Services Union Treaty of 1967.

The Entente, under the leadership of the Ivory Coast, is attempting a similar pattern of economic integration. On an even wider scale, the UDEAC (UEAC) and OCAM aim at economic and technical integration of French-speaking states — with very limited results to date, however.[4]

Of greater importance have been the trade and aid ties with former metropolitan countries and, to a limited extent, the new relations with the great powers, the United States, Soviet Union, and China. The former colonial powers deliberately have encouraged policies of close economic cooperation with their former dependencies. Most African states have responded favorably to this initiative, with varying results. The associative status of former French territories with the European Economic Community is the clearest example of this policy. So successful has it been that several former British colonies, particularly Nigeria, have worked out a similar relationship.[a] The effect of this relationship with Europe has been to emphasize the old trade and aid ties with France and, regardless of other benefits, this has made the integration of African economies far more difficult. The political effect, therefore, has been to reinforce regional differences within Pan-Africanism.

This kind of integration raises very large questions. The patterns of trade continue to run outward, like the spokes of a wheel. Integration is achieved

---

[a]Nigeria was the first to reach an associative agreement signed in July 1966. She obtained trade benefits, but not investment participation.

through the financial capitals of Europe, and not through Ouagadougou and Nairobi. Nevertheless, the long-range tendencies are toward political regional affinity in Pan-African relations. There has been a general increase in intra-African trade. Collaboration is growing in African bargaining with external units such as the EEC, and technical cooperation was proven beneficial.

These regional units are not all stable subsystems. In terms of our primary criteria, the Maghreb (Algeria, Tunisia, and Morocco) has had only fleeting unity. The UAS of Ghana, Guinea, and Mali has been laid to rest quietly. And both the larger blocs, known as Casablanca and Monrovia, have passed from the scene for reasons to be discussed shortly. OCAM, though a very significant political alliance, lacks the economic and political consistency of a functioning regional subsystem.[5]

To date, only three systems appear to have much future — the East African Common Service Organization, UDEAC, and the Entente. The common services and marketing program is the strongest linkage in each case. Each possesses a certain political cultural identity, a loose problem-solving mechanism, and varying degrees of autonomy.

The Entente is the least nonaligned of the three; the East African system is the most nonaligned. Both the East African and the Central African systems include radical states, indicating that even ideologically oriented nonaligned states do not find such integration impossible.

Functionalism and Federalism

A major point of debate over the form of Pan-Africanism has been functionalism versus federalism. The federalists, led by Nkrumah, minimized the differences among the new African states and urged the formation of an "All-African Political Union," with real political powers to coordinate foreign policy, defense, and economic development.

The functionalists opposed this structural approach to unity and proposed gradual step-by-step integration through economic and technical commissions, prior to any political fusions. The controversy over the road to African unity frequently became highly charged ideologically during the years preceding the formation of the OAU.

Often political disputes, such as Pan-African policy in the Congo crisis, became embroiled in the debate. Ideological considerations were frequently raised. The Nkrumahists accused the functionalists of contributing deliberately to the division of Africa and of seeking favors from the neo-colonialists. In turn, the functionalists accused Nkrumah of wanting a unified Africa in order to fulfill his messianic complex.[6] They argued that such a step would be premature. The late Prime Minister Balewa of Nigeria pointed out that most African states had enough difficulty ruling themselves and wondered how they could successfully broaden this to include others. Nkrumah replied with the simplistic notion that most internal differences of African states resulted from colonial influences.

First unify Africa in an All-African Political Union, he maintained, and then an Africa strong enough to keep out the great powers and abolish disunity among African brothers will appear.[b]

To the credit of most African leaders, they were not persuaded by Nkrumah's utopianism. Not even some of Nkrumah's closest African associates, such as Sékou Touré, ever believed seriously that a union government could be created as a first step in the unity of Africa. Guinea participated in the original Ghana-Guinea union, and then later, with Mali, in the UAS because of such benefits from Ghana as the initial $20 million loan.

Nkrumah and some of his extreme left Pan-African advisers, such as A.K. Barden of the Bureau of African Affairs, used the ideological appeal of governmental union very effectively in the politics of Pan-Africanism. This group attempted to build support across Africa for their revolutionary approach to all African problems. They were successful especially among students and trade unionists. A growing group of political exiles from various African countries responded, also. These comprised two categories: refugees from the unliberated territories of southern Africa and various groups working in exile against their own independent governments. Nkrumah's revolutionary ideology became a rationale for struggling against their incumbent governments. Their enthusiasm was stimulated further by the support Nkrumah gave to an amazing array of revolutionary groups operating out of Ghana.[7]

All this was carried on under the sacred banner of Pan-Africanism. Leaders threatened by Nkrumah's Pan-Africanism, such as Houphouet-Boigny in the Ivory Coast and Sylvanus Olympio in Togo, were stirred to wrathful action. They sought to organize counter-Pan-African forces against the revolutionaries. Togo, especially, gave sanctuary to Nkrumah's exiled opposition, such as Dr. K. Busia. Sympathy and surreptitious support also came from those Western powers that felt their interests were threatened. The United States was particularly concerned about the scope of communist complicity it believed was part of the intrigue stemming from Ghana.

These rivalries were among the major motives behind the emergence of three regional groups prior to the Addis Ababa conference in 1963. These groups have been analyzed fully in numerous studies by Colin Legum, William Zartman, and Claude Welch, among others. Their significance in the regional Pan-African rivalries needs to be mentioned here, for their history is linked to the OAU and the pattern that came after them.

The first of these was the so-called Brazzaville Group formed by a conference of twelve French-speaking states at Brazzaville in October 1960. As leader of the Council of the Entente, the Ivory Coast took the initiative in convening the Brazzaville Twelve: Niger, Upper Volta, Dahomey, Cameroun, Central African Republic, Chad, Congo (Brazzaville), Gabon, Malagasy, Mauritania, and Senegal.[8] This group founded the Africa and Malagasy Union, which was pro-French, functionalist, and against the revolutionary approach to nonalignment and Pan-Africanism. They opposed Morocco's claims on Mauritania. On these issues as well as on recognition of Communist China and on the Congo

[b]Nkrumah presented these views in many works.

crisis, their thinking was aligned closely with that of France. At that time, these French-speaking states were so dependent upon France that they could not qualify as nonaligned, even under the most flexible, pragmatic definition. This situation changed following the formation of the OAU and the successor group called OCAM. Several members of this group, especially Congo (Brazzaville) and Chad, became more radical on nonalignment and Pan-Africanism.[9]

Thus, from the time of the Sannequillie Declaration (July 1959), when Nkrumah and Tubman fell out, the Pan-African movement was divided badly despite all attempts by its proponents to minimize their ideological and political differences.

In response partly to the conservatism of the UAM and partly to the more radical stance of African states regarding developments in Algeria, the Congo, and Mauritania, the Casablanca Group came into existence in January 1961. Although invitations are said to have gone to a much wider list, only five heads of state took part in the initial conference: Ghana, Guinea, Mali, Morocco, Egypt, and the head of the Algerian Provisional Government.[c]

The Moroccan king, Mohammed V, convened this group because he was then seeking allies against the French creation of Mauritania from territory claimed by Morocco. Both Egypt and Ghana were canvassing for support for the Algerian government-in-exile and for Lumumba's government in the Congo. In addition, Nkrumah thought he saw the potential beginning for a union of African states and persuaded the Casablanca powers to draft a Charter of Independent African states, later adopted by only five states. As in the case of the UAM, certain functional commissions were created in the areas of defense, economic development, and culture. None of them ever operated effectively, and political differences finally shattered the group.

Casablanca failed to become the basis of African unity because of the revolutionary nonaligned views shared by the founding participants. Morocco was for a number of years an active participant, despite her conservative, monarchic form of government. However, her new ruler, Hassan II, after the outbreak of hostilities with Algeria in 1964, moved toward a pro-Western position in search of military backing.[10]

Many of the remaining independent African states, feeling that their international policies were not adequately represented by either Casablanca or Brazzaville, took the initiative to form a third group that came to be known as the Monrovia group, after the capital of Liberia, where the first meeting was held in May 1961.

The politics of Pan-Africanism was not consciously bloc-formation, and therefore all the independent African states were invited to the first conference at Monrovia and the second at Lagos, in January 1962. The nature of the group, however, was determined by those who attended. The french-speaking Brazzaville Twelve elected to participate, while the Casablanca Five, after initially accepting invitations, decided to boycott when the Algerian government-in-exile was not admitted. The Monrovia group, like the other two, drafted a charter, established a number of commissions, and passed anti-colonial resolutions. The

[c]Libya participated but later withdrew.

major concerns expressed were: 1) assurance of the territorial sovereignty of existing African states that felt under pressure from the revolutionary designs of Morocco and Ghana, in particular; 2) condemnation of atomic testing "anywhere in the world"; 3) economic sanctions against South Africa; and 4) support for the Central Government of the Congo (Leopoldville) then under the leadership of President Kasavubu.[11]

The Monrovia Group held several meetings between 1961 and 1963 and disbanded its formal structure when the OAU was constituted in 1963. Like the Casablanca Group, cooperation was minimal between meetings of the heads of state. The diversity of background was very great. When it became apparent that these minimal functions of political consultation and economic and technical cooperation were to be assumed by an all-encompassing group, the OAU, Monrovia disbanded.

The continental spirit of Pan-Africanism more than anything else undermined the separate identities of Casablanca and Monrovia. Functionalists and Federalists found minimum agreement in their aspiration to establish a unifying, all-encompassing African system. They shared an unsophisticated faith in the proposition that they had much more to unite them than to divide them.

Many saw the launching of the OAU as the beginning of a new era. Hopes were very high that Pan-Africanism had triumphed over the divisiveness at last. Many of these hopes were doomed to failure as the price of all-inclusiveness often became inconclusiveness. Yet, from another perspective, something very significant for Africa was begun at Addis with the founding of the OAU.

The Organization of African Unity

Many different interpretations of the significance of the OAU exist among African leaders as well as foreign observers.

During the founding conference, a new spirit swept over delegates. Even Presidents Tubman and Nkrumah embraced each other in the presence of the rejoicing heads of state and governmental representatives from thirty-two African countries. Nkrumah, on his return from the summit conference, hailed the new charter with the words, "We are united at last."

Actually, Nkrumah was attempting to cover over the failure of his own position on Pan-African unity. The Addis conference marked the triumph of functionalism over federalism in Pan-Africanism, and of pragmatism over the radical approach in nonalignment. Nkrumah and the other African revolutionaries recognized this, and, after a brief period of official harmony, returned to their tactics of revolutionary intrigue through their own network of Pan-African contacts.

The OAU differs very little in form from the regional organizations that have marked the postwar era, from the Council of Europe to the Arab League. It has been thoroughly studied, so only the major points are touched upon here.[12]

The plenary powers are in the hands of the Annual Assembly of the heads of state. But most of the work is done by the Council of Ministers that usually meets several times a year and considers matters prepared for its agenda by the permanent secretariat under the leadership of Secretary-General Diallo Telli of Guinea.

Unlike many regional organizations, the debates usually are held in private session and no verbatim reports are issued, making analysis of policy differences difficult. However, the first six years of the OAU's experience suggests certain conclusions regarding its role.

The basic differences among the African states have not disappeared with the creation of a unity structure. These differences have led to confusing resolutions and inconsistent support during the major crises that have come before the OAU, such as the Congo and Rhodesia. These will be discussed in Chapters 4 and 5. There have been one or two minor successes on temporary issues such as the Moroccan-Algerian border war of 1964. A ceasefire and temporary settlement resulted mainly from the personal diplomacy of Emperor Haile Selassie of Ethiopia. Yet the OAU arbitration commission clearly assisted in working out the details of a temporary compromise.

The OAU has achieved some success in the less controversial fields of technical and economic agreements. While not directly responsible for the origin of the African Development Bank, the OAU did help foster its emergence. The Scientific, Technical and Research Commission absorbed, in 1965, the old Committee for Technical Cooperation in Africa (CCTA), which had a staff of 100. The new Commission rivaled the Secretariat itself. The Economic and Social Commission has impressive plans to study the restructuring of international trade, the development of intra-African trade, the coordination of the means of transportation, an African payments and clearing union, an all-African monetary area, and the harmonization of national development schemes. These studies, when completed, will be useful, although the political problems of implementing them are more formidable than their initiators envision.

Probably the OAU's most important Pan-African undertaking has been in the limited coordination of national support for liberation movements in southern Africa. Its African Liberation Committee (The Committee of Nine) has had significant resources at its command. Under the original agreement of 1963, OAU members were to allocate one percent of their national income to its program. The actual contributions have not been disclosed, but reliable estimates place the figure much lower. The allocation of these resources has been a source of tremendous controversy, primarily because of the rivalry among the liberation groups in the same territories and among various territories. This situation will be discussed in detail in Chapter 6. Nevertheless, several of the major liberation groups probably would not have been able to operate without the OAU commission headquartered in Dar-es-Salaam. The limits of African resources are not the only problems the commission faces in supplying materials and training as well as funds. Effective allocation of this support has been complicated by the differing policies of the nine members of the commission. Liberation politics never can be separated fully from internal considerations in the OAU's member states or from their policies toward the great powers.

The Revival of Regionalism

No important aspect of the OAU's work has been free from the relationship of African states with outside powers. Pan-Africanism cannot be separated from individual problems. In every situation, delegates are forced to review the effect of a stand at the OAU upon their own weakness and sources of external support.

Therefore, although all the various pre-1963 regional groupings were dissolved, the initial enthusiasm over solidarity has been revived in new form. There remain three major caucus groups, each possessing a certain core of members whose governments and policies have had greater stability than others. Rivalry is continuous among these groups and constantly threatens the unity of the African subsystem organized around the OAU.

The most formal of these groupings is the former Brazzaville members, who have created the OCAM as a successor to the UAM. Initially, the OCAM was not intended to serve the same regional political functions of the UAM, but was meant to implement further the functional arrangements of its technical branch, OAMCE, which was never discontinued. The OAMCE was established in 1961 to maintain and extend the intra-African functions of banking, currency, transportation, and telecommunication. It has been the most successful of all such technical agreements among African states, building on the trade, financial and communications pattern laid down previously by French administration.[13] Attempts to extend this pattern to other African French-speaking states (Togo, Cameroun and Rwanda) have been only partially successful. And negotiations with the English-speaking states of West Africa for participation in aspects of technical cooperation such as the Benin Union, involving Nigeria, Dahomey, Togo and Ghana, have had negligible results.

This inner-directed technical cooperation was given an outer-directed political push in 1965 at the Tananarive Conference, under the leadership of the Entente of Ivory Coast, Niger, Upper Volta, and Dahomey. Several motives lay behind this step. The participants were convinced that affiliation with the European Economic Community had been highly successful and they wanted to fend off political attacks from exiles collectively and improve their positions *vis-à-vis* the EEC. The old UAM group had continued to caucus at the United Nations. Probably the most important concern was increasing fear of revolutionary pressure on their governments given support from an external base in Accra. Counter-pressure against the revolutionaries seemed necessary.

Opinion in the OCAM group, however, differed considerably. They are divided between radicals like Chad and Mali, moderates such as Senegal, and conservatives led by Houphouet-Boigny. These political divisions have weakened its effectiveness as a subsystem in Pan-African and nonalignment politics.

An illustration of the political difficulties and weaknesses of the group was the attempt by the Entente to boycott the 1965 meeting of the heads of state of the OAU in Accra. These four states bordering Ghana charged her with protecting and training revolutionary groups for international subversion of independent African states. They maintained that they could not make a friendly visit to a country harboring their enemies and called upon all other members of the OCAM group to boycott the meeting.

Prime Ministers Balewa of Nigeria and Senghor of Senegal attempted to arbitrate the dispute for they feared a major boycott might destroy the OAU. Finally, Nkrumah agreed to deport objectionable political refugees from Ghana during the conference and the protesting states were asked to submit names of "undesirables." Ghana apparently honored the agreement, in part, but this did not satisfy the Entente, which, joined by Togo, Gabon, Malagasy, and Chad, did not attend the meeting.

Severe criticism was directed at the boycotting states for threatening African solidarity. A byproduct of the meeting was a resolution defining the status of political refugees, which is a widely recognized legitimate role among African single-party authoritarian systems. Each leader must hedge against the day when he may be in exile. Even President Tubman, with the longest record of continuous rule in West Africa, expressed the hope that if ever he were a political refugee he would not wander homeless in Africa.[14]

The Accra Heads of State Conference almost became the breakingpoint for the OAU, although unity was restored later, particularly after Nkrumah's fall. But basic rivalries lie just below the surface of the African system, threatening even minimal functioning.

A second distinct group in Pan-African politics is also diverse, corresponding very closely to the revolutionary nonaligned, discussed in the last chapter. The membership of this group has changed as a result of changes within the individual African states. Ghana dropped out after the military coup in 1966, while several others have joined. New additions include Tanzania, Congo (Brazzaville), and Somalia, with Burundi in and out. The Sudan was temporarily under the revolutionary transition government of October 1964-June 1965. At the time of the Stanleyville drop, Uganda and Kenya were also temporary members.

Tanzania has gravitated into this group over the years, though Nyerere has remained independent. He is a revolutionary in Pan-African affairs, but shuns involvement with the revolutionary "positive neutralists" on a world scale. This distinction is important for a number of African states. They agree on African issues such as the Congo, but not on matters of strategy in such crises as Cuba, Berlin, or Vietnam.

The hard core of the radical group consists of the Arab states of North Africa (minus Tunisia and Libya) plus Mali and Guinea. Algeria, despite the deposition of Ben Bella, has remained a working, though more introverted, member. This group has very little functional integration as their economies are separated widely. A common sense of alienation from the Western powers, and for most, an internal revolutionary fervor appears to hold them together. Their critics maintain that this derives from their acceptance of economic and military support from the communist world. Certainly, this type of support is characteristic of their development patterns, but it fails, by far, to explain their conduct completely.

Somalia has joined this group because of her irredentist struggle with Ethiopia, Kenya, and France. Her major support comes from her Arab friends of the North. Russian backing has slowed as a result of the Franco-Russian detente. (France seeks to restrain Somali influence in the area around Djibouti). To a limited extent, the Chinese have filled this gap, though they, too, are sensitive to Kenya's views because of their growing involvement in East Africa.

So far, this group has not sought to create any formal institutional framework within Pan-Africa. They operate as an informal caucus, consulting and cooperating as issues arise.

The third group is even more diffuse. It consists of countries who feel neither functionally related to OCAM nor ideologically drawn to the revolutionaries. Their view, in many ways, reflects the amorphous pragmatism of the old Monrovia cluster. The membership is widely drawn across the continent, from Lesotho to Tunisia. They seldom take the initiative, except when an issue concerns them directly, as in the case of Zambia versus Rhodesia, and Uganda reacting to the pressures from the Congo in 1964.

Much of the weakness of this middle group arises from lack of leadership. Each potential candidate has been disqualified by individual problems. Nigeria, long the leading candidate, has been eliminated by internal strife, as has been the Congo (Kinshasa). Zambia is too young and is caught on the horns of her economic dependency on Rhodesia. Tunisia is both uninterested in and subject to pressures from Algeria. Ethiopia is the only member of this group with the internal strength and international prestige capable of giving it direction. However, although Haile Selassie is respected, Ethiopia, because of her reactionary domestic political system, is not.

Thus, the middle group of Pan-Africans fragmented into a number of tendencies, all contradictory, which pulls it in different directions. Many are swing states: the Sudan aligns with the UAR on Arab issues; Kenya guards her East African and Commonwealth ties; Rwanda is drawn to OCAM: Chad belongs to OCAM, but feels more ideologically in harmony with Mali; Malawi is caught in the crossfire between economic dependency on white supremacy in southern Africa and the pressures of liberation movements based in Tanzania.

Nevertheless, this middle group has served an important function. It provides a buffer zone between the extremes within the OAU. Members of this group have attempted to provide arbitration services in such disputes as the tragic Biafra War in Nigeria.

Rivalries between the caucus groups threaten to destroy the system constantly. Yet, they have not done so in the years since the OAU was founded in 1963. This fact indicates that the African subsystem is a reality.

Strength of the Subsystem

The fragmentation of the OAU has reduced the effectiveness of the African nonaligned subsystem considerably but has not destroyed it. Despite the rivalries of the regional subsystems and caucus groups, the OAU continues to exist, perhaps partly as an unfulfilled wish, like the United Nations, but also because it reflects at a certain level the operation of the basic components of any international system. Despite the apparent differences among African cultures and races, they are drawn together by a consciousness of common brotherhood and identity as Africans. Prime Minister Abubakar Balewa, who was among the most practical of African leaders and was not given to flights of fancy over Pan-Africanism, summarized the reality of this African identity in the following categories:

1. a common historical experience of the impact of Western Europe,
2. a similar cultural heritage in art and craft, no less than in social and spiritual values,
3. a readiness to welcome and accommodate new ideas, a burning desire for progress and a profound belief in the efficacy of human effort,
4. a natural candour which is allied to a strong sense of fair play and justice,
5. a capacity for surviving arduous conditions even where these include the deliberate infliction of hardship and cruelty,
6. above all, an irrepressible sense of humour and gaiety, of charity and hope.[15]

Not all of these categories are distinctly African, yet taken as a whole, they summarize the substance of the African personality.

The OAU record for solving problems is bleak, but not barren, as demonstrated by the mediation of over a dozen different disputes from the Moroccan-Algerian to the Tanzanian rebellion. The creation of the African Development Bank as well as other integration agencies and important studies of African development potential are relevant to the problem-solving that must go on if the African system is to continue to evolve. Attempts to support liberation movements have been weak, yet perhaps their sponsorship and funds have been vital in the actual initiation of many of these movements.

The greatest accomplishment of the OAU might well be its self-policing to keep the great powers out of direct intervention in Africa. As the next chapter will show, this failed in the Congo Crisis of 1964, but the constraint on the great powers in a number of potentially explosive conflicts from Morocco to Zanzibar and Rhodesia has been great. Intervention continues but is limited by African collective opposition to certain forms.

The growing autonomy of Africa is seen more clearly in the development programs of individual countries and the growth of functional regional schemes such as the East African Common Service Organization. The diversification of aid in both military and economic categories as further evidence of this trend is discussed more fully in Chapter 7.

The impact of regionalism has been to diversify the pattern of African nonalignment. Each regional system is nonaligned in its own way. Insofar as their differing interpretations of nonalignment have come into conflict, they have weakened the overall system; but this has not always been the case. French intervention in Gabon in 1964, for example, was seen as a general threat to the

African system, especially by the Francophone states. This threat resulted in negotations with France by the leaders of the OCAM group that have made this kind of intervention less likely in the future.

Regionalism could become a threat to the overall African system if one or more of the caucus groups should fall under the domination of a great power and be utilized by that power to forward its objectives in Africa. Despite the differences between the regional groupings, this has not happened so far. The prospect that conflict among African states will break out and involve great powers is, of course, constantly present. This prospect is the greatest threat to the nonalignment subsystem, since Africa with its immense ethnic, racial, and irredentist pressures is continuously on the brink of the break down of order. Clearly the greatest danger stems from the white-dominated areas that are, in fact, extensions of great power influence in the nonaligned continent. Pan-African writers have not been wrong about the potential for conflict from this source, not only between Africans and Europeans but also among African states themselves.

Conclusions

Pan-Africanism is an early ideal of African nationalism that remains unfulfilled. But the reality to which it has given birth is a nonaligned international subsystem that functions in spite of regional systems and caucus groups that often conflict with it.

With the wisdom of hindsight, this is not surprising. Pan-Africanism as a continental movement was really only unified in the anti-colonial struggle. Racial identity and concepts of 'negritude" are meaningful at best only for a minority of the continent's inhabitants. The fact that significant unity of action has been achieved primarily on "liberation" issues illustrates the major anti-colonial origins of the movements. Such realistic conclusions, however, should be qualified by future prospects. Only a cynic would exclude the possibility of greater unity and, ultimately, even the dream of all-African political unity being achieved.

The implication for nonalignment is clear. As long as the African subsystem can be maintained against internal and external pressures the significance and prospect of nonalignment are enhanced. If the system is broken, the chances that certain African states would align with great powers would be enhanced. However, even in this case, independently functioning nonalignment systems might arise either from the regional subsystems or even from one of the caucus groupings.

The danger of conflict among the African states is minimized by the continuance of the OAU pattern. African leaders recognize this fact and great powers, at least the United States and Soviet Union, are not anxious to see the African peace broken. Should this happen, the centripetal forces of conflict would tend to pull great powers into the center. Thus, the great power desire for African allies is tempered by their fears of triggering conflict among themselves over areas that are marginal to their security.

White Intervention and Black African Reaction: The Case of the Stanleyville Drop

In large measure, nonalignment is designed to prevent great-power intervention in African politics. Yet, intervention broadly defined is taking place all the time and this keeps African relations with outside powers in a constant state of tension.

At times, the nonalignment pattern has been nearly broken permanently by acts of military intervention. However, the breach has been repaired and the pattern restored, indicating that the system has a great deal of resilience and absorptive capacity.

The real problem is to distinguish the kinds of intervention that are tolerable and can be absorbed by the nonalignment system from those that tend to destroy it. Intervention must be defined more broadly than the use of direct military force by outside powers. In the African context, it means the use of major political or economic as well as military force by the great powers to influence the policies of African states.[1]

Frequently, foreign aid has been cited as a form of intervention. Aid and loan agreements usually have terms that influence the direction of economic growth or trade in favor of the interests of the donor. Political leaders and factions of political groups receive favoritism and support, overt and covert, from great powers. Great powers may even participate in *coups d'etat*. Obviously, this form of intervention is intolerable to Africans if it comes to public attention. Yet, the instability of African governments invites such intrigue. Africans call this intervention neo-colonialism.

The form of intervention that is recognized universally as most intolerable to nonalignment is the employment of military force by outside powers, particularly the former colonial powers. Since direct conflicts of interest do arise in the post-colonial period, it is important to consider the circumstances in which such intervention takes place and the consequences of such intervention for the nonaligned subsystem. The outstanding case to date has been the Beglian-United States-United Kingdom intervention in the Congo in November 1964, known as the "Stanleyville Drop."

The Congo Crises

The Congo has been a central issue in the development of African international relations, and has influenced the character of African nonalignment substantially. There have been two major crises to date. The first was important as an example of multi-lateral intervention under the auspices of United Nations peace-keeping. The second was a tripartite Western intervention which met widespread African resistance.

The First Crisis

The origins of the first Congo crisis have been analyzed at great length by other scholars.[2] The international character of the United Nations peace-keeping intervention was its most important aspect, and the intervention was characterized throughout by international legitimacy and regional cooperation. Both the Monrovia and Casablanca African groupings supported the UNOC intervention initially. The Congolese government, after Lumumba's fall, cooperated closely with the UNOC forces.

There were, however, points of intense friction. The radical African states supported the Lumumba government against Kasavubu, whom they considered to be under neo-colonial control. The moderate African governments and Western governments backed Kasavubu. A key issue was whether the United Nations peace forces should be used as an offensive force against the Katanga army or should limit their operation to maintaining order. The radicals pressed for offensive action, while the Western states sought to limit the scope of operations.

When the Russians began to attack the UNOC directly, several radical African states, particularly Guinea and the UAR, withdrew their support. This intensified the Cold War aspects of the dispute and very nearly destroyed the effectiveness of United Nations intervention. However, the tragic death of Dag Hammarskjöld, the Secretary General of the United Nations, resulted in a shift of power toward the Afro-Asian grouping in the United Nations and under U Thant's leadership, offensive action was undertaken that forced Katanga's capitulation.

Thus, despite the Cold War tensions and the views of some African leaders that the tolerable boundaries of outside intervention had been exceeded, the international character of the UNOC was preserved. Without the legitimizing role of the United Nations, many other African leaders undoubtedly would have turned against this intervention as a violation of the rights of independent African states and the concept of African nonalignment. The attitude of Nkrumah is illustrative. He personally persuaded Mali and Guinea not to withdraw their troops from the United Nations peace-keeping operation at a meeting of the Casablanca Powers in January 1961.[3] Later, Mali and Guinea did withdraw, but Nkrumah kept his troops in the Congo despite serious clashes between Ghanaian troops and the Congolese government forces under the command of General Mobutu.[4]

A great many questions have been raised about the effectiveness of the United Nations intervention. Obviously, it did not resolve the basic issues, for shortly after the last United Nations forces departed in 1964, the second crisis broke. However, the method of intervention received the support of most African states. It complied with their conception of nonalignment and international relations.

The Soviet world was antagonized by the action as was a section of the West. Yet, the action received sufficient support of major groupings in the international system to make it work. Despite the relative success of the UNOC, this same formula was not employed in the second Congo crisis.

The Second Crisis

The second Congo crisis had important new elements within it. It was precipitated by the rebellion of tribal factions, partially supplied by communist sources. Western powers intervened without international or regional sanction. The government of the Congo, which requested intervention, was headed by a leader whose credentials were suspect in the eyes of most other African states because he spearheaded the earlier Katanga secession.

The northern province of the Congo around Stanleyville was a troubled area from the time of the independence of the Congo. This area was Lumumba's home base, where he started his national movement, the MNC (Movement Nationale Congolais). Naturally his defeat and death caused great bitterness among his followers. After Lumumba's departure from the scene during the first crisis, his lieutenant, Antoine Gizenga, became the leader of the hardcore Stanleyville province.

As Vice-Premier of the Congo, Gizenga claimed to be the legitimate Prime Minister, after Lumumba was imprisoned "illegally" by Mobutu and Kasavubu. He established his capital in Stanleyville and set out to reunite the Congo under his rule. For a brief period he received support from communist and revolutionary African governments. Ghana, for example, retained emissaries in both capitals of the Congo until the Leopoldville government ejected Nathan Wellbeck, Nkrumah's representative.

The reconvening of Parliament in July 1961 offered a basis of compromise acceptable to Gizenga. The Congo River blockade and the refusal of the Sudan and the East African states to permit outside powers to supply Stanleyville, plus the capitulation of Tshombe and the rise of a compromise government under Cyrille Adoula, with MNC participation, cleared the way for reunification.

The Stanleyville group was reconciled briefly to a new, united Congo after the defeat of the Katanga secession. One of the MNC leaders, Christopher

Gbenye, became Minister of the Interior under Premier Adoula, although he was virtually a prisoner in the intrigue presided over by the skillful Premier.

For several reasons this arrangement did not last. The politics of the Congo has always been exceedingly unstable, due to the intrigues of tribal groups and personalities. Outside forces from East and West engaged in continuous intervention in pursuit of what is considered the richest prize of Africa. Probably the single most important factor in the disaffection of Stanleyville from the Leopoldville government was tribal politics, based on a long history of ethnic rivalries and messianic sect conflicts of that area.

The basis of tribal unrest was centered among the Batetela-Bakusu of Maniema and Sankuvu. These were Lumumba's own people, and he became the symbol of revenge for the leaders and insurrectionist groups of the area. Virtually all the officers of the Armée Populaire de Libération (APL) came from this group.[5] An uprising over a succession dispute among the Bafulero on the Burundi frontier was the event used by the radical rural leader Gaston Soumialot to seize the first important urban center in May 1964. He began to move from the rural areas into the urban centers.

As soon as the agrarian rebels showed some success, they were joined by the more ideological political refugees based in Brazzaville. In 1963, Christophe Gbenye and other fugitives from the Adoula government set up a Comité National de Libération (CNL). This CNL group had no cohesive ideology and was riddled by factions, each claiming to be the legitimate heir of Lumumba. In contrast to the Soumialat movement, their tactics were those of *coup d'etat* rather than revolution.

In the spring of 1964, after the initial success of the rural leaders in the northern province, the political exiles left Brazzaville to help establish a "People's Republic of the Congo" proclaimed in the Stanleyville province. This alliance of the sophisticated professional politicians and the rural militants of the APL was very uneasy. For example, Thomas Kanza became Foreign Minister of the People's Republic of the Congo only for a few days and then, appalled by the ruthless practices and constant maneuverings of the rural leaders, General Olenga, Soumialot, and Mulele, departed for exile again.

The Western press made much of the communist origins of the Stanleyville rebellion. The story was incorrect and contributed substantially to the differences of policy between Western powers and African states.

The only major figure among the leadership who had any extended contact with communism was Pierre Mulele. He had studied for an undetermined period in Communist China, and on his return to the Kwilu province in 1963, began to organize forest bands in the region of the Bapende and Bambundu. Other leaders adopted communist slogans and sought to imitate, in crude fashion, the rural revolutionary tactics so successfully employed by Mao Tse-Tung in China. Among these practices was the liquidation of captured, educated officials of the Leopoldville government. Assassination and terror is not a tactic confined to Communists, but they have demonstrated its effectiveness on a wide scale in

Asia, and African revolutionaries from the Mau Mau in Kenya to the rebels in the Congo have not hesitated to adapt it to their ends.

The Chinese Communist embassies, and those of the Soviet Union, based in Brazzaville, Burundi, and East Africa, were by no means disinterested spectators. Undoubtedly at times they supplied money and arms to the Stanleyville rebels. But, as Colin Legum of *The Observer* (London), among others, has documented, this was a trickle compared to the support the Western powers poured into Leopoldville.[a]

The logistics of supply alone limited communist operation. They could use no direct route from Brazzaville. Indirect routes across East Africa through Tanzania and Uganda were available for a short time. The Sudan offered a supply route briefly, following the October 1964 revolution. This was discontinued after being interdicted by the Southern Sudanese rebels who were eager for arms.

Insofar as the Stanleyville rebellion had an ideology, it was atavistic revolutionary nationalism. Lumumba was its patron saint, and the enemy was Western imperialism attempting to transform the Congo into a client state of international mining consortiums and finance capital. The Leopoldville government, first under Adoula and later Tshombe, was hated bitterly as the perverter of Congolese unity established under Lumumba and as wholly corrupted by the bribes of Western interests.

This world view in Stanleyville saw the Chinese and Russians as allies in the struggle against Western imperialism. They also identified with the revolutionary African states of the Casablanca powers to whom they added Kenya, because of Kenyatta's close association with Mau Mau, and Tanzania, for its increasingly revolutionary stance after the union of Zanzibar and Tanganyika.

The policies of the Leopoldville government contributed to the alienation of the northern rebels in several ways. The Adoula government never succeeded in winning the confidence of any Stanleyville leaders, from Gizenga to Gbenye. Adoula could not control the army, which on many occasions prior to the rebellion engaged in severe reprisals, extortions, and massacres in the Stanleyville, Bakwana, and Manono areas. The Congolese army was not "a true national force."[6] The central government capitulated to its threats continuously, and local government in the North was unstable.

Political party control was never reestablished after the formation of the Adoula government. After Parliament was reconvened in 1962 to approve his new cabinet, Adoula dismissed the elected representatives. The real control of the Congo then fell into the hands of the famous Binza Group.[b]

The Binza Group, in turn, was beholden to the immense interests of Belgium and the United States. And when Adoula could no longer control the factions of intrigue, or the spreading rebellion in the North, these interests brought Moise Tshombe back from exile to rule the Congo in mid-1964. Almost simultaneously, the last restraining link to the post-Katanga crisis settlement was severed with the departure of the few remaining United Nations peace-keeping forces.

---

[a]United States financial and military support of Adoula and then Tshombe was extensive. Most significant were the planes and Cuban pilots supplied by the CIA.

[b]The key members of this group were General Joseph Mobutu, President Joseph Kasavubu, and Victor Nendaka, head of the secret police.

The installation of Tshombe as Premier further aggravated the suspicions of the rebels concerning the nature of interests behind the Leopoldville government. Reactivation of the Katanga army and the re-employment of white mercenaries from southern Africa and Europe to lead the ANC convinced a wide circle of Africans, both in the Congo and outside, that whatever the shortcomings of the brutal tactics of Soumialot and the communist associations of Mulele, they held more promise for the future of the Congo than Moise Tshombe.

Thus, a combination of reactionary influences, Army excesses, ambitious political intrigue and the general breakdown of central government authority contributed substantially to the tribal power-base on which the initial success of the Stanleyville rebellion was built.

The Stanleyville Government

The People's Republic of the Congo was proclaimed in the spring of 1964 and lasted only three-and-a-half months. At its high-water mark in August, it controlled over half the Congo. It had the sympathy, though little support, of the communist world. Moreover, most African states had refused to recognize Tshombe as the head of the Congo state. Its forces, "the Simbas," defeated the Congo Republic's army, the ANC, in every engagement, and it appeared they would be in Leopoldville before the end of the year. Yet, they never made it. Their final defeat was more the result of their own unrestrained, brutal practices than the power of outside forces.

Thomas Kanza was the most widely respected of the Stanleyville officials, as he had been Ambassador to the United Nations for Gizenga's government and had represented Adoula in Great Britain. Few other well-educated leaders and none of the students at the Lovanium University joined in the insurrection. However, the real power in the Stanleyville government was held by the agrarian rebel leaders rather than by the CNL political leaders. Although the MNC was revived and replaced the CNL as the official party, its political leadership under Gbenye could not restrain the self-appointed generals and colonels of the People's Liberation Army.

The purges were both official and unofficial, and went on continuously. In these bloody pogroms that frequently turned into savage public disemboweling scenes, the educated and experienced group, capable of giving some administrative efficiency to the government, was gradually eliminated. Self-appointed vigilante groups roamed the streets of Stanleyville and numerous other urban centers, executing anyone suspected of some "Americanism." Eventually, as with most purges, they turned on themselves and several of the more able rebel leaders, such as Francois Sabiti, were swallowed up in their revolution. It is estimated that at least 20,000 persons were liquidated.

In this hysterical atmosphere, a number of Europeans, including missionaries and traders, were imprisoned and executed. The Western press described in great detail the beating of priests and raping of nuns, who were then thrown to the crocodiles. But the stories were highly exaggerated; probably 200 Europeans were killed. The Western press gave the impression that the revolt was primarily anti-White, whereas the main fury of the tribalists was directed against Westernized Congolese.

These bloodbaths were a major reason the rebels failed. They weakened the control the original rebel leaders had established over several areas, such as Elizabethville. The populations and local leaders turned against them, and by September 1964 Tshombe's mercenary-led and well-equipped ANC forces had turned the tide of battle and were marching on Stanleyville.

The Stanleyville Drop

The most controversial event in the entire episode occurred on November 24, 1964. American planes took off from a British base and dropped Belgian paratroopers on Stanleyville. To most African governments, this was unjustified outside intervention in an African civil war. But to the British, American, and Belgian governments, it was a mercy mission to save the lives of hundreds of Europeans held hostage by the Stanleyville government. The incident brought into focus the whole issue of the legitimacy of military intervention and the power and role of the African nonaligned system.

The brief facts of the incident are these. The Stanleyville rebels were facing defeat with the advance of Tshombe's mercenary columns, who were exacting a heavy reprisal price on the populace as they approached the rebel capital. Gbenye blamed the defeat of his Peoples Liberation Army on the support given the ANC by the Western powers. Therefore, in desperation, the rebels rounded up several hundred Europeans and announced they were hostages. If the West did not intercede with Tshombe to halt the advance on Stanleyville, Gbenye threatened to shoot all the expatriates in reprisal.

For several weeks, the United States resisted both domestic and European pressures for immediate intervention. It hoped that the OAU might find a basis for resolving the impasse between the two rival Congo governments. Most African states felt that this was not a matter for the United Nations or the great powers, but an African dispute. A commission of the OAU under President Kenyatta of Kenya had been created and was actively seeking to mediate between Gbenye and the West.

Earlier attitudes in the OAU of almost complete rejection of Tshombe, demonstrated by the refusal of the Cairo Heads of State Conference of the OAU, in July 1964, to even hear him, had changed by September, when he was given a hearing at an emergency session in Addis Ababa.

African states, however, were divided badly over the crisis. The moderates, led by Nigeria and Senegal, advocated an African force be brought in as an intermediary while an election was held. The more revolutionary Africans feared that such a force might be used against the rebels and supported conciliation among the various factions inside and outside the Congo. An all-night session behind closed doors decided to establish an *ad hoc* commission to consist of Cameroun, Ethiopia, Ghana, Guinea, Kenya, Nigeria, Somalia, Tunisia, the UAR, and Upper Volta, with President Jomo Kenyatta as Chairman. The task of this commission was 1) national reconciliation within the Congo, 2) the normalization of relations between the Congo and her neighbors, Brazzaville and Burundi, whom Tshombe charged with supporting the rebellion.

By consultation with the various factions, the Kenyatta Commission hoped to devise a solution to the widening conflict that was threatening to involve great-power intervention. The commission visited Brazzaville and Bujumbura and obtained promises of cooperation. However, the collapse of rebel resistance before the rapid advance of the ANC left little time. The African leaders still hoped that an agreement could be reached when the Western powers decided to act.

Belgian paratroopers were lifted into Stanleyville and quickly freed most of the expatriates, but could not save approximately sixty, including the now-famous missionary, Doctor Larsen. The American planes airlifted some 1,500 refugees to Leopoldville, and within forty-eight hours the operation was completed. A few hours later, the ANC arrived and quickly occupied the city. This effectively ended the rebellion, although the rebel forces attempted to resist for several months, utilizing the sanctuaries of neighboring states, the Sudan and Uganda.

The Aftermath

On few occasions has such an outpouring of anti-Western feelings swept Africa as in the aftermath of the Stanleyville Drop. Moderate and pro-Western leaders felt compelled to denounce the precipitous Western "imperialist intervention." President Kenyatta was "appalled" at the action. President Nyerere went much further and compared it to Japanese action at Pearl Harbor.[7]

The more revolutionary pro-Marxists exploded in verbal wrath, recalling the worst pages of colonial history and charging racialist motives on the part of the Western powers. C. D. Ganao, the representative of the Congo (Brazzaville) said in the Security Council debates on the issue, "The Stanleyville agression . . . has just proved in a striking fashion that there is no place for the black man in this world, wherever he may be, whether it be in a country to which he came in the same way as others before him, or in his own homeland of Africa."[8]

In the aftermath of the "intervention" in many areas of Africa, no non-African could feel safe as the mobs surged through the streets attacking, stoning, and burning. This writer was in Khartoum at the time and vividly remembers sleepless nights waiting for an evacuation order.[c]

A few moderate African leaders sought to defend the action of Western powers. Prime Minister Balewa of Nigeria viewed the action as a necessary humanitarian step which was undertaken at the request of the Congo

---

[c]The United States Embassies in all crisis-ridden areas have such plans for its nationals. This, in itself, is an example of the unequal relationship the Africans were protesting over Stanleyville. If race riots were to threaten the lives of foreign nationals in Washington, D.C., would the United States grant foreign powers rhe right to evacuate their own nationals?

government. However, his was a lonely voice among Africans, most of whom had not recognized the legitimacy of the Tshombe government to speak for the Congo.

In time, however, the harsh antagonisms softened, as most of the pragmatic governments came to accept the Leopoldville government. Even a number of the revolutionary governments who had directly aided the rebels and given them sanctuary were soon disillusioned with their factional quarrels and obvious inability to control any significant area of the Congo.

The Lessons of Stanleyville

The direct intervention at Stanleyville by Western powers touched the sensitive nerve of nonalignment attitudes among most of the African states. As might be expected, the more revolutionary African states reacted most violently. But few Africans, even today, are prepared to agree with the Western governments that the action was necessary.

The major issue turns on the matter of legitimacy of this level of intervention. The more moderate are prepared to accept the reality of the continued Western interests in an important and rich area such as the Congo. They are even prepared to accept, at least privately, the necessity for indirect subsidies and assistance for political groups in times of instability, especially when communist influences are attempting to take advantage of such crises. But they cannot accept direct military intervention on behalf of an African government with as questionable representative credentials as those possessed by Tshombe at the time he came to power in 1964.

Tshombe was widely regarded as an instrument of international financial interests in the abortive Katanga secession. And his employment of White mercenaries from South Africa and Rhodesia further inflamed the smoldering racial tensions of the African continent.

African antagonism was aggravated by the fact that most African states had not come to accept the Tshombe coup. Their view of Tshombe was very similar to the British view of the Smith regime in Rhodesia. While it was *de facto* in power, it had not been given *de jure* acceptance. Several African states were campaigning actively to devise an alternative to the Tshombe government.

By involving the Congo in international intrigue and cold war conflict, many African leaders felt the Tshombe government compromised everyone else's nonalignment. From the standpoint of Africa, Tshombe was an unnecessarily provocative agent who could not be restrained. If left to destroy itself, the Stanleyville government would probably not have seized Western hostages.

Intervention in General

There have been other instances of Western military intervention in conflicts within African states. The cases of Tanzania, Uganda, Kenya, and the Gabon can be cited. In each case, the duly constituted government that had succeeded colonial rule had requested the former metropolitan power to intercede on its behalf against insurgent army groups.

Several important differences between the Congo and these cases must be noted. Most important was the absence of the Cold War issue. The French intervention in the Gabon had some Cold War aspects, for the rebels certainly were less pro-Western than the Mba government; but in East Africa the rebel soldiers had no outside ideological connection or support. Secondly, the action was undertaken by closely related former colonial powers who were requested to intervene by well-established governments. Moreover, these governments were all legitimate governments in the OAU system, and the members of the OAU generally support this means of dealing with military rebels.

In this connection, it should be noted that France and England have refused several requests to intervene. The most famous was de Gaulle's refusal to rescue President Abbe Youlou of Congo (Brazzaville) from a leftwing coup. The British turned a deaf ear to the Kabaka of Buganda when this traditional monarch requested aid against the central government of Milton Obote.

Thus, it is clear that outside powers apply other criteria than whether a request comes from a legitimate authority. Considerations of the consequences of intervention in terms of the overall interests of these powers are weighed carefully.

Conclusions

Great-power military intervention in African conflicts runs contrary to the nonalignment system of the African states. They are prepared to accept intervention for the purpose of retaining a legitimate government. However, this is strictly limited to cases where no wider issues such as the Cold War or conflicts between African states are involved.

The second Congo crisis revealed the reality of the nonalignment system when the Cold War issue was present. Moderates and radicals united to protest the intervention. The only important African leader who defended the Western action was Balewa of Nigeria. The inability of the African system under the OAU to resolve the issue without intervention is due partially to its weakness but also must be seen in the light of the precipitous use of power by the intervening states. If the Kenyatta Commission had been given more time, the problem-solving mechanism of the OAU may well have succeeded in forestalling external intervention. This, after all, was its primary objective. The Stanleyville government was already falling apart.

Thus, when the Cold War is a clear-cut issue in the African mind, the nonaligned subsystem is stimulated into action.

Western concern for the safety of nationals is understandable. International law has long covered these matters. With the consent of the government concerned, evacuation of nationals has been recognized. Yet, the political consequences of such action within the nonaligned system must be weighed against the exercise of national rights. In this case, it seems the Western governments not only failed to assess the weaknesses of the Stanleyville rebels but also failed to recognize the toleration limits of the African nonalignment system.

Because of the emotional ethnocentric aspects of this crisis, there has been very little objective assessment, even among Africanists. Even scholarly questioning of the necessity for the United States intervention touches sensitive religious and patriotic sentiments. I believe that we must learn to accept searching criticism and analysis of our foreign policies in the same way reasonable men accept analysis of domestic politics.

From an impartial and reasonable examination of the facts it does appear the Western powers acted precipitously and from motives more related to the Cold War than to saving lives in the Stanleyville intervention. The end result would not have been significantly different, in terms of the defeat of the Stanleyville rebellion, which was already well under way. There is no certainty that all of the hostages would have been massacred. And if the principles of nonalignment had been more fully respected, the world might have been spared a dangerous and ugly crisis.

The question of international legitimacy in interventionary action is very important here. Whenever regional or international agencies, such as the OAU, are attempting to act in such a crisis, it is not a suitable occasion for direct intervention. The instance of United Nations peace-keeping in the first Congo crisis demonstrated the utility of international legitimacy. In the second crisis, the Western powers failed to gain the support of the African states and, therefore, resorted to their own measures of force, with highly unsatisfactory consequences.

A greater respect for the reality of the African nonalignment subsystem can, in the future, prevent such serious conflicts of interest. This does not mean that Western powers should not pursue their interests and try to protect their nationals in dangerous situations. Nevertheless, they must pursue them with greater restraint; and by other means that are more tolerable to the dignity and the procedures of African self-rule.

The wisdom of this direction has been recognized by the nonaligned policies of the Mobutu government that overthrew the pro-Western Tshombe government. Gradually and painfully the Congo (Kinshasa) has been reducing its dependency upon the West and has sought by symbol and policy to draw closer to the center of nonaligned African policy. This has been necessitated by the continuing ethnic instability within Congo politics and the intense competition of external powers for control and influence over this wealthy area of Africa.

General Mobutu faces an immensely difficult task. Yet he has been able to rally some former Lumumbists to the task of creating a wider political base. He recognizes that the Congo cannot be nonaligned as long as it remains militarily and economically dependent exclusively upon the West. By the nationalization of industry and the removal of American influence over the military, he has begun to move toward a new position for the Congo in African and world politics.

Another Congo crisis may well test again the fabric of such policies. However, the general recognition of the legitimacy of nonalignment may preserve the Congo from the same intense civil war pressures of the first two crises.

5 The Coming Confrontation Over Race: The Rhodesian Case

The Rhodesian white settler government, with its dependence for existence upon South Africa and trade with the Western world, represents everything the new African states most oppose through their nonalignment policies. A racial confrontation with the gravest implications for the future of nonalignment on the African continent is emerging out of this strong African reaction against Rhodesia.

When race is the issue, there are two basic subsystems in Africa. The cleavage is not as sharp on other issues; but, as James Rosenau has suggested, when we identify issue areas, the lines of a subsystem clarify sharply for us.[1] Black nonaligned Africa constitutes one subsystem and the white dictatorships of southern Africa are the major states of a second subsystem. Associated with this white subordinate system are a few black African states, such as Malawi, Lesotho, Botswana, and Swaziland, who are dependent in varying degrees upon southern Africa. This white-dominated system is subordinate to the Western world economically, militarily, and culturally.[2] Although a nominally independent identity is maintained, it has little substance. The West is frequently embarrassed by this close kinship relationship because of the racist character of the regimes of the subordinate system. Significant trade is almost exclusively Western, with the exception of Japan and South Africa. External investment, on which their economies are dependent, is Western; and their military supplies and training come from the Western world. There is growing interaction between these southern African countries, but there is very little interaction with the Communist world. Thus the southern African system is not significantly autonomous or independent. It is, as a political system, in the Portuguese phrase, "an extension of Europe in Africa."

If this is true, can these states resist the measures taken against them by the Western world? At this writing, these measures have dealt only with the forms of power and not its reality. United Nations resolutions do not disturb this reality as long as arms supply continues through NATO. Rhodesia continues to trade with the outside Western world and the United Kingdom through South Africa. South Africa and the United States have military agreements for the use of ports and air bases. If the West were to cut off these relationships the white subsystem would rapidly collapse because of its dependency.

As the African nonalignment system has emerged, conflict has increased between it and the Western, white subordinate system of southern Africa. This conflict presents a threat both to the peace of Africa and to the relations of nonaligned Africa with the Western world, as the latter are inevitably drawn into the confrontation.

This potential conflict raises many questions concerning the future of nonaligned Africa. Can the nonaligned system deal effectively with the southern system that at present appears far more powerful? What will a conflict with the West (in its support of the southern subsystem) invite in terms of new Cold War intervention? As the conflict grows, will internal differences divide the radicals and moderates among the African states and sharpen the rivalries already exerting powerful disintegrating pressures on the African subsystem?

The Rhodesian crisis has been the crucible of conflict in which the boundaries of divergent interests between the two systems have become clearly discernible. By tracing the origins of the Rhodesian racial crisis within the country itself, among the African states, and in the international arena, we get a clearer picture of the major dimensions of the problem.

The white subsystem with its Western links has supported the Rhodesian government of Ian Smith. The African subsystem, because of its influence within the international system as a whole, has become the primary agent for raising the issue and pressing the conflict.

The outcome will largely determine the future of Africa. Thus, the apparent shadow-boxing of antagonists is only an ominous symbolic preliminary of future real confrontation.

Unilateral Declaration of Independence (UDI)

Former British colonial territories have made unilateral declarations of independence without bringing down British power and the United Nations against them. The Sudan declared itself independent on January 1, 1956, and India did the same in 1947. The Rhodesian declaration of 1965, however, was clearly different from the former two in that it denied the majority of its citizens the opportunity to participate in the power and benefits of its political system.

In Rhodesia, power was seized by a minority claiming a special civilizing mission, but practicing an odious form of racial discrimination. This aroused the opposition of the British government, and the hostility of the independent African states who, despite their differences over means, agreed in opposing the continuation after independence of a South African type of racial system.

The white Rhodesians declared themselves independent of Great Britain on November 11, 1965, in a unilateral declaration that was recognized neither by the British government nor by any other state in the world, although South Africa maintains a *de facto* relationship. The whites simply seized power, motivated by the fear that Great Britain was preparing to introduce new constitutional measures that would give more power to the black African majority.

White Rhodesians were able to accomplish this *coup d'état* because of their long-standing control of the instruments of force in the Crown Colony and because of their special historical relationship with Great Britain. Their bond with England was not simply racial, though that was important — it was an involved and distinctive social, economic, and cultural relationship.

Africans, especially the Matabele and the Mashona had occupied Rhodesia for many centuries before the English came. In the latter part of the nineteenth century, immigrant white settlers, mostly English rather than Afrikaner, came up from the Transvaal in South Africa under the leadership of Cecil Rhodes. Moreover, Rhodesia, with its attractive highlands, became a favorite point to which Englishmen immigrated directly from Great Britain. These included a significant group of upper-class retired colonial officials, military officers, and landowners, opposed to the socialization trend in England.[3] At the time of UDI only 31.5 percent of the white Rhodesians were native born. Thus two-thirds of the whites immigrated after 1945.[4]

In 1923, the white settler group had become numerous and prosperous enough to successfully demand self-government. Great Britain agreed to internal self-government, and handed over to the handful of Europeans Parliament, the civil service, the police, and the armed services who would rule themselves and the three million or more Africans.

Because of the property and education requirements, the only Africans permitted to vote and participate were a few immigrants from South Africa.[5] Great Britain reserved the authority to protect the rights of Africans under the 1923 Constitution. However, the British government never employed this power. Rhodesia was given a Governor-General and was placed under the Commonwealth Relations Office, rather than the Colonial Office.[6] Thus, since 1923, the whites of Rhodesia have enjoyed a status of self-rule and commonwealth participation little different in practice from the other "white dominions" of the Commonwealth.

The Racial Basis of Power

Much has been made of the point that Rhodesian racial attitudes are considerably different from South African. While the differences are basic, a strong working relationship between the two countries has existed and has been consolidated during the Rhodesian UDI crisis.

The Rhodesian system is racial in practice, though not officially racist in doctrine. The majority Rhodesian view has never been based on the apartheid doctrine that Africans are inherently inferior to Europeans. Most Rhodesians have agreed with the dictum of Cecil Rhodes: "Equal opportunity to civilized men and equal opportunity for all to become civilized." The difficulty has lain in determining the standards for "civilized" life. The white settlers have tended to raise these standards increasingly as a growing number of Africans became educated and entered the modern economy. The A and B rolls for voters have been the means by which African participation has been restricted.[a] This practice is systemic racism, since African participation in the political system is controlled by ethnocentric and European standards of the whites that presume African inherent inferiority.

Prime Minister Ian D. Smith indicated that equality was a matter of generational change when he said, "We will never negotiate with Britain while Mr. Wilson is in his present position because he is waiting for us to reach the position of one man, one vote, and this will not happen in my lifetime or Mr. Wilson's."[7] Two racist concepts that have characterized European rule from the very beginning are implicit in this statement. First is the assumption that European-derived standards are necessary for civilized life and self-determination. The assumption that European methods of education and systems of wealth production are necessary preliminaries for self-determination is not shared by many newly independent states in Asia and Africa.

The second racist assumption is that Africans cannot acquire these standards in less than several generations. This presumes that even a crash educational program would not effectively bring the African into the modern political system. Such an assumption is more clearly racist than the first, because it is based on a social Darwinian view of inherently inferior African learning ability. Racism is predicated on alleged genetically derived differences in the abilities of certain groups of people. While the majority of Rhodesians would not maintain that in theory the African is inherently inferior in his abilities, they have created a cultural racism which sets European standards as the norm and maintains circumstances in which the African cannot attain these standards. This policy is systemic racism.

The Practice of Systemic Racism

Systemic racism is social discrimination against identifiable racial groups on the basis of alleged hereditary characteristics. We are familiar with this type of stratification according to racial castes in the United States. In the less complicated social system of Rhodesia, Africans have long been segregated in special schools, reservations, and types of employment and social services. Much of this has been necessitated by the underdeveloped character of African society and their different culture, but that does not explain all of it. An African child of the Mashona tribe will have to attend a primary school to learn English and other aspects of the Rhodesian European-dominated society before he can move into the same stream of education as a white child. But this does not explain why ten times as much money should be expended on a white child as on an African, or why all European children are required by law to obtain a secondary education while less than 2 percent of the African children have entered secondary school.[8]

[a]High property and education standards are required for the A roll. Since European standards are much higher than African, they control the A roll by a margin of 10-to-1. The majority of seats of the Parliament are chosen from this roll. Over the years, European governments have simply raised the requirements.

Education is only one way social opportunity is stratified by race in Rhodesia. Land has been divided between the races since the land Apportionment Act of 1930. Prior to that time, Africans could freely acquire land anywhere. Since then, less than 10 percent of the population has been entitled to own over 50 percent of the arable land, and Africans were disqualified from owning property in the cities. As in South Africa, the role of the African outside the reserves was to serve the white man. Labor regulations came into effect, limiting his opportunity to acquire a skilled profession. Even on the land, the African was restricted by measures like the Land Husbandry Act which controlled the crops he could raise.

If the social discrimination of separate housing, recreational and public services are added to this picture, the principle of equal opportunity becomes a hollow mockery. Recent modifications, such as integration of the University College of Salisbury, have been only minor concessions to obtain external assistance from the United Kingdom. The vast majority of Rhodesia's citizens remain victims of a system of racial segregation and economic exploitation. Whether economic motives or social prejudices have been the underlying motives cannot be determined fully. However, the racial character of the system, the kinship with and growing dependence on South Africa, have become unfortunate realities known throughout Africa, and have precipitated intense counter-racial sentiments among Africans.

Internal African Nationalism

African nationalism developed late in Rhodesia due to the authoritarian control of the settler governments. The brief interlude of the Central African Federation helped to stimulate nationalist activity in the fifties. By 1960, Joshua Nkomo's Zimbabwe African People's Union (ZAPU) was demanding majority rule in the government.

The British responded to African nationalism with cautious support. However, most settler leaders grimly determined on a course of suppression. When England pressed for a moderate change in the Constitution that would increase African participation, the moderate government of Sir Edgar Whitehead fell, and Smith, with his strongly racist Rhodesian Front, rose to power. A referendum in 1961 on a new constitution, although strongly opposed by ZAPU, was adopted. The Rhodesian Front came into existence with the specific purpose of gaining independence *prior* to African majority rule. The statements of its leadership in the 1964 campaign left no doubt about this objective.[9] The United Kingdom opposed this trend, but faced counter-pressure and finally the settlers' rebellion of 1965.

The history of Rhodesia has been marked by a direct correlation between the degree of British liberalizing pressure and the extent of bitter settler extremism. The racial fears of the majority of the settlers have consistently precluded compromise. To many observers, UDI ended the illusion that the Rhodesians intended, even ultimately, to build a genuinely multiracial society. Margery Perham perceived correctly that the Rhodesian settler attitude was affected in large measure by events in other parts of Africa. "Their scorn for Britain's surrender, as they saw it, to African violence is linked with this reading of the total African scene . . . of all the negative lessons they drew from the stormy prospect of the north, none has been more horrifying than the events in the Congo."[10]

Sanctions Against UDI

The British government's negative reaction to UDI was based primarily on the illegal seizure of power. Also, a sense of the importance to the United Kingdom of African racial feeling was a strong supporting motive.[11] However, Prime Minister Wilson resisted strong African pressure to attempt to put down the UDI rebellion with force and chose instead to utilize diplomatic and economic sanctions. The basic assumption in this decision was that a powerful group of liberal Rhodesians would oppose the Smith regime out of loyalty to Her Majesty's government and a concern for their businesses and farms. This calculation of the Wilson government overestimated the extent of opposition to Smith among the settlers. Nevertheless, the original step had been taken and, as with many such fateful decisions in affairs of state, the course had to be pursued to its uncertain end.

The most precise definition of British initial objectives in opposing UDI was issued as a result of the "Tiger Conference" between the two Prime Ministers. From this conference came the six basic principles of NIBMAR (No Independence Before Majority Rule):

1. The principle and intention of unimpeded progress to majority rule, already enshrined in the 1961 Constitution, would have to be maintained and guaranteed.

2. There would have to be guarantees against retrogressive amendment of the Constitution.

3. There would have to be immediate improvement in the political status of the African population.

4. There would have to be progress towards ending racial discrimination.

5. The British government would need to be satisfied that any basis proposed for independence was acceptable to the people of Rhodesia as a whole.

6. It would be necessary to ensure that, regardless of race, there was no oppression of majority by minority or of minority by majority.[12]

Initially, Wilson hoped the United Kingdom could defeat UDI within a few months by the application of oil sanctions that would threaten industry and agriculture in Rhodesia. South Africa and Portugal easily undercut this campaign by smuggling oil through the token British blockade.[13] The African states intensified their demands for the use of force, but again Wilson concluded that economic sanctions could provide a solution if they were widened, under the auspices of the United Nations, to include all nations. On December 16, 1966, the United Nations Security Council invoked mandatory sanctions under Chapter VII of the Charter, for the first time, with a vote of 11 to 0. France, Mali, Bulgaria, and the Soviet Union abstained.[14] Several African attempts to strengthen the resolution through the inclusion of a ban on coal exports to Rhodesia were rejected; but the adopted resolution placed a mandatory ban on asbestos, iron ore, chrome, tobacco, pig iron, sugar, copper, meat, hides and skins, in addition to oil. The sale of all military equipment to Rhodesia was also banned. All member states were urged not to facilitate trade or financial support for "the illegal racist regime of Rhodesia."[15]

This broadened sanctions program did not have the anticipated effect for several reasons. Most serious from the standpoint of the British strategy was the tendency of Rhodesian whites to unite in support of the regime under attack. This appeared to result from a combination of patriotic feelings aroused by the international pressures and a general belief that the sanctions could not be enforced. Externally, a number of states even extended their trade with Rhodesia, rather than comply with the United Nations ban. Not only did South Africa and Portugal, who had an ideological stake in violating the United Nations request, extend their trade, but France, Iran, Japan, and West Germany all increased their trade with Rhodesia in 1967, reflecting their contempt for international principles.

A high proportion of the loss of British trade was taken up by Western European countries. Johan Galtung, in his article "On the Effects of International Sanctions,"[16] considers diplomatic as well as economic sanctions, and makes a percentage estimate of the degree of compliance by various regional groups and countries. These conclusions are based on information available in March 1966 and, therefore, are very limited. But they show a surprising degree of African noncompliance with economic sanctions. His conclusions, in general, are:

1. Zambia (export sanctions 30 percent effective)
2. South Africa (export sanctions 0 percent effective)
3. West Germany (export sanctions 70 percent effective)
4. Malawi (export sanctions 0 percent effective)
5. United States (export sanctions 45 percent effective)
6. Congo, Leopoldville (export sanctions 0 percent effective)
7. Portugal & territories (export sanctions 0 percent effective)
8. France (export sanctions 50 percent effective)

There is considerable controversy concerning the real origins and extent of these violations. However, second and third parties have been used skillfully by importers and Rhodesian exports moved through South African and Portuguese ports under forged labels, with false certificates of origin. British nationals were implicated extensively in violations. One report from the Portuguese indicated that 58 out of 169 oil tankers which called at the port of Lorenço, Marques between April 1966 and May 1967 were of British nationality in the service of British companies.[17] The Portuguese figures were denied by the British authorities, but *not* the fact that a number of British tankers were violating the ban.[18] Other instances of individual British, French, and other European companies violating the ban were reported in the British press, indicating widespread forgery and blackmarket operations in London, Paris, and Tokyo under the cover of South Africa and Portugal. A prominent American mineral firm, Union Carbide, was implicated in the *London Sunday Times'* exposure of oil-supplying to Rhodesia. The Rhodesian semi-secret agency, GENTA, shipped 110,000 gallons every 24 hours from South Africa; and Union Carbide, through its British subsidiary, Rhodesia Chromes, Ltd., facilitated the Portuguese shipment of 140,000 gallons a day from the refineries in Lorenço Marques.[19]

Most important was the practical support South Africa gave Rhodesia. The Rhodesian pound was underwritten by South African banks. South African companies purchased large quantities of Rhodesia's chief export crop, tobacco. South African police and military forces have participated in counter-insurgency operations on Rhodesian soil. The supply of oil by road from South Africa played a major part in helping Rhodesia break the oil blockade.

Without South Africa, despite the sympathy of Portugal and, to some extent, France, the Rhodesians probably could not have withstood the sanctions campaign. This act of complicity by South Africa against the international legal and moral sanctions of the United Nations ranks in international annals with the surreptitious French and British sabotage of the sanctions imposed by the League of Nations against Italy in 1936. Ironically, Africans have been the principal victims of these failures of international economic sanctions.

The sanctions campaign had some real effects on the Rhodesian economy. By the end of 1968, serious inflationary pressures and profit losses with grave long-term implications for the economy were evident. One economist estimated a 15 percent fall in real income of the settlers. Stagnation had become a prospect because net capital formation had fallen nearly 50 percent.[20]

However, because the immediate objectives had not been achieved, the Wilson government was criticized by the Right for undertaking the campaign and by the Left for failing to enforce it rigorously. Therefore, by the end of 1969 Wilson was looking for a face-saving way out. The conference on "The Fearless" in October 1968 showed that the British government no longer insisted on NIBMAR. The idea of majority rule before independence was dropped.[21] In its place the Wilson government proposed a "blocking system" with appeal provisions to the Privy Council to prevent cutbacks in African rights. This formula would nominally restore British sovereignty, but would leave the settlers firmly in control of the rate of African growth in power and participation. The "Fearless Proposals" were rejected by all contending groups in Rhodesia, though a small center group of businessmen and African moderates supported them. If adopted, the formula would have allowed for British pride and accommodation to Rhodesia, but its suggestion opened even wider the gap between the United Kingdom and the African states.

The Internationalization of the Issue

The temper of the debate at the United Nations showed rising African frustration with the ineffectual measures against Rhodesia, as the real British intent was suspect. The British were accused of secretly trying to protect their "kith and kin" in Rhodesia and of not being serious about international sanctions. Thus, racial feelings appeared. The role of the United Nations itself as an agency for effective social change was questioned. Most serious of all, feelings grew in African capitals that the United Nations had become a device for diverting African revolutionary challenges to the system of white domination. The *Times of Zambia* summed up this feeling after the Kitwe UN Seminar on Apartheid and Racial Discrimination: "The end result of this may well be disillusionment with the United Nations to the extent that the Afro-Asian nations no longer consider it a worthwhile organization. Such a reaction could lead to a confrontation between black and white in Africa."[22]

The individual African states most directly affected by UDI obviously were too weak to deal with Rhodesia themselves. Therefore, they sought to rally "Pan-Africa" under the auspices of the OAU, against Rhodesia and her allies. They invoked the principles and power of the United Nations on behalf of their cause. The racial issue they saw in UDI pulled together the divergent interests of the African members of the nonaligned subsystem into a pattern of unanimity and cooperation unprecedented since the Congo crisis of 1964.

The warnings of African leaders that Rhodesia was about to declare UDI were not taken seriously by Western governments. A year previous to UDI, the Council of Ministers meeting in Addis Ababa, September 5-10, 1964, stated in a resolution that they were "perturbed by the intentions of Mr. Ian Smith's government to declare independence unilaterally so as to keep the majority of the people disenfranchised." They called upon the United Kingdom to convene a constitutional conference and impose a system of "majority rule, on the basis of one man, one vote."[23] However, the OAU and the world were primarily concerned with the Congo crisis, and Rhodesia only received secondary consideration. At this stage, the African states most concerned with the issue were Zambia, Tanzania, and Uganda.

Increasing African concern over Rhodesia was demonstrated in the speeches of African leaders in the fall of the following year at the United Nations General Assembly and in the Second Ordinary Assembly of the Heads of State at Accra, October 12-25, 1965. At the Accra meeting, the major principles of African opposition were laid down and received unanimous support from the attending heads of state. Several francophone states such as the Ivory Coast were not present, but at the United Nations, shortly thereafter, the Ivory Coast revealed her complete support for the substance of the Accra resolution of the OAU.[b] Differences concerning the the tactics of dealing with UDI appeared later.

The Accra resolution deplored "the refusal of the United Kingdom Government to meet with firmness and resolution the threat of a Unilateral Declaration of Independence" and requested the convening of a constitutional conference and the release of all political prisoners, such as Joshua Nkoma and Ndabaningi Sithole, who had been detained a year earlier. On the eve of UDI, the African states requested all states to withhold recognition, and then resolved to: a) reconsider all political, economic, diplomatic and financial relations between African countries and the United Kingdom government in the event of this government's granting or tolerating southern Rhodesian independence under minority government; b) use all possible means, including force, to oppose a unilateral declaration of independence; c) give immediate assistance to the people of Zimbabwe with a view to establishing a majority government in the country.[24] After the Rhodesian UDI, a special session of the OAU Council of Ministers convened in Addis Ababa. The action of this meeting demonstrated both the intensity and the frustration of the African leaders. Unable to muster the strength necessary to intervene militarily themselves, they sought to pressure the United Kingdom into using force. The resolution drawn up by the OAU Ministers placed the responsibility for dealing with the rebellion upon the British. In order to exert maximum pressure upon Great Britain, the African states unanimously agreed to withdraw diplomatic recognition if the British failed, by December 15, 1965, to use force to put down the rebellion.

Shortly after the foreign ministers returned home, many of them discovered how impractical such drastic retaliation against Great Britain would be. President Kenyatta was one of the first to indicate that his country did not approve of this victimization of the United Kingdom, but preferred to take the issue to the United Nations. Only nine of the thirty-five OAU members at the Addis meeting carried out some diplomatic withdrawal action. These nine were all among the radical nonaligned group, indicating the significance of ideological considerations to these particular nations. Tanzania, especially, exemplified the intensity of this factor since she had a great deal to lose in terms of British economic and technical aid.[25] Although Zambia was most directly affected by UDI, she remained so dependent upon the United Kingdom financially and economically, that she could not undertake a diplomatic break with the British, as President Kaunda announced in Lusaka on December 7, 1965. Her policy reflected the underlying pragmatic considerations of most members of the OAU, who realized quickly the futility of trying to force the British government to undertake a step it had rejected for a number of its own considerations (of which opposition by the British public to the use of force was a major one).

Why did the OAU Council of Ministers seriously adopt such an extreme proposal that was shortly to make them appear ridiculous and the OAU futile? The decision was not taken hastily or without the consent of many of the heads of state, as most of the presidents had been present at Accra in the preliminary

[b]The Ivory Coast introduced a resolution that was pressed to a vote, requesting the consideration of the invocation of Chapter VII of the United Nations Charter.

decision on a possible diplomatic boycott.[26] Nor were the delegations guilty of bad faith and sheer opportunism. This writer was present during this special session of the OAU and noted an unusually deep current of anti-British feeling among the foreign ministers, based on the belief, as one diplomat put it, that "the British were conniving with the Rhodesians" and secretly intending to head off the threat of African majority rule. This basic suspicion toward British integrity on the Rhodesian issue has colored the feelings of virtually all African leaders of all political persuasions.

These suspicions were aroused by the long history of United Nations debates on Rhodesia, in which the British continually resisted African pressure to submit information about Rhodesia and declare it a proper matter for United Nations concern. As the African writer B. Vulindlela Mtshali noted, "Why was Great Britain unwilling to grant in Rhodesia what she has granted elsewhere in Africa? Was it because Rhodesia was ruled by white people closely related to Britain? From the start, this suspicion underlay the United Nations debates."[27]

As in the Stanleyville crisis of 1964, the deep racial suspicions of the Africans concerning Western integrity were again aroused over the UDI crisis. At such times, African leaders are swayed at least temporarily by the more emotional policies of revolutionary ideologists. In this case, most African states did not rupture diplomatic relations with Great Britain totally because of very powerful pragmatic considerations. However, for a few, such as Tanzania, the Sudan, and Congo Brazzaville, it was a major step toward complete alienation.

The United Nations and Sanctions

The initial British attempt to deal with the situation by its own program of oil sanctions against Rhodesia brought African scorn for its inevitable failure and an increasing demand for United Nations action.

In May 1966, the African states made a concerted effort to bring the issue to Security Council consideration, under Chapter VII, "as a threat to peace," but were blocked by the determination of the United Kingdom to keep the matter within its own jurisdiction. At this point, Britain argued that Rhodesia was neither a non-self-governing territory nor an independent state, but had a special status and relationship to the United Kingdom that she alone could settle. Her position was supported indirectly by seven abstentions (Argentina, China, France, Japan, the Netherlands, United States, and Uruguay). The Mali-Nigeria-Uganda resolution to invoke mandatory sanctions was supported by only six votes.[28]

The tension between the African states and the British was eased somewhat by the end of the year, when the United Kingdom, after a final ultimatum to Rhodesia had lapsed, took the issue to the Security Council under Chapter VII, as "a threat to peace." The historic resolution invoking mandatory sanctions was passed.

The step was well received in Africa, but did not convince most African states that anything less than the use of force would achieve the desired result. They were also convinced that both South Africa and Portugal would support the Rhodesians against the sanctions of the United Nations. Therefore, they felt that retaliatory action in the form of sanctions should be brought against these countries as well.

This pessimistic view of developments was borne out by events. As noted previously, extensive underhanded support was supplied to Rhodesia to circumvent the worst effects of sanctions. Consequently, the African leaders returned to their campaign for more stringent measures (including the use of force) at the United Nations. In June 1967, at the Kitwe Seminar of the United Nations on Apartheid and Racial Discrimination and Colonialism in Southern Africa, attended by thirty-two governments (not including the United Kingdom), the first clear outline of this new program appeared.

The Seminar requested that sanctions be made "total, comprehensive and mandatory," and requested the creation of a group of experts under the Secretary-General to enquire into the effectiveness of sanctions. They called upon the United Kingdom to "crush" the Rhodesian government with force, and requested retaliation against South Africa and Portugal for aiding Rhodesia by sanctions and the withholding of arms. The participants, with some reservations from the United States and Japan, asked for support of the liberation forces, in terms of material and moral aid.[29]

These views were carried with increasing militancy to the United Nations. The Africans won the overwhelming support of the General Assembly in a sharp debate with the British. The resolution of the Fourth Committee was adopted 90 to 2, with 18 abstentions. However, the United Kingdom was backed up by all the noncommunist Western states. "The Committee condemned the failure and the refusal of the United Kingdom as the administering power to take effective measures to bring down the illegal racial minority regime; called upon the United Kingdom to enter into consultations with the representatives of political parties favoring majority rule; condemned the continued support given the regime by South Africa and Portugal; called for the immediate expulsion of South African armed forces from Southern Rhodesia; . . . and urged all states to render moral and material aid to the national liberation movements of Zimbabwe."[30]

Ghana, Kenya, Sierra Leone, and Tanzania all suggested it was important to find some way of making South Africa and Portugal comply with the Security Council sanctions decisions. The issue of British complicity was raised again by the pro-Western Liberians, who suggested that the United Kingdom by the assurance that it would not intervene militarily had encouraged the Smith regime to rebel.

Malawi and Botswana were the only African states to speak against the resolution.[31] These two small African states are dependent upon South Africa and Portugal, and reflected this dependency in their views questioning the use of force as an effective means. Their emergence as critics of African militancy marked the first break in African solidarity on the Rhodesian issue.

While the United States and the Scandinavian countries did not share the

British optimism about the effectiveness of sanctions, they also did not favor the Afro-Asian Communist bloc call for the use of force. The South Africans and the Portuguese were the only two votes against the resolutions, and both denounced the accusations against them as false. Thus, the United Nations, by the end of 1967, had reached another impasse between African demands for stronger measures and Western views that harsher measures could not bring the desired results.

Prospects

During early 1968, the United Kingdom took a stride toward the African position that temporarily raised hopes that they were coming together. These hopes were greatly dampened by the "Fearless Conference" and indications that the United Kingdom intended to abandon the active sanctions program.

The Security Council Resolution of June 1968 imposed comprehensive mandatory sanctions for the first time and created a committee to examine reports of the Secretary-General on the implementation of the resolution.[32] This resolution did not go so far as the Afro-Asian states desired, for it provided exceptions in trade and immigration. But the major issue remained the use of force. No enforcement provisions were included, though inspection procedures were established.

Despite British tendencies to settle with Rhodesia rather than press the sanctions campaign, the issue had become international. The African states were determined to oppose any settlement short of the overthrow of white supremacy. Thus the gulf had become, by the end of 1968, wider than ever.

The British fear the consequences to their own economy of using force that would bring them into a showdown with South Africa. Moreover, there has been very little public support in Great Britain for the use of force against Rhodesia.[33] There has been only minority sympathy for United Nations involvement. In addition, surprisingly little concern has been shown for African reactions. The Conservative Party opposed the resort to sanctions and, in October 1967, demanded that a settlement be made with the Rhodesian government.[34]

Prime Minister Wilson went as far as English public opinion would permit him to go. Even if he had wished to use force, he faced opposition in the country that might have brought down his Government. English provincialism and even race-consciousness in this matter is an unfortunate fact. Yet, one wonders how other Western peoples would have reacted under similar circumstances. This is the basic substance of the confrontation between races and ways of life that is coming in Africa.

If the United Kingdom comes to terms with the Rhodesian Government on the basis of what appears to the Africans to be a sell-out, the consequences to African-British and African-Western relations will be severe. Emotional ideological considerations will become paramount to some African states; while pragmatic considerations could exert a restraining influence on others, though few African governments can afford to appear to condone a policy of accommodation with the Smith government. Prime Minister Kenneth Kaunda would appear to be speaking for many African leaders when he said at the Kitwe Conference that "white racialists in Rhodesia have seized power from an apparently feeble and decidedly hesitating British Government," and that "The Rhodesian crisis" had "exposed British policy in Africa."[35] This growing distrust could lead to a break between the United Kingdom and some of the African states whose interests are most directly involved.

The Rhodesian crisis clearly has had the effect of consolidating the African states on this issue. It reaffirms the basic pattern of the African subsystem on the race issue. The Soviet Union and communist states generally have joined the African system on the Rhodesian question, but the latter have been the prime movers. Africans have tried to keep the Cold War from confusing the issue and weakening United States support for their proposals. Thus, the initiative has been primarily a nonaligned one based on African interests, and opposition to racism in any form.

This situation is subject to rapid change, however, if communications between certain African states and the United Kingdom break down over the issue. The radical pattern of behavior of certain ideologically charged countries has been noted already. These states are most supportive of the liberation movements. If they break their connections with the West and turn to the Communist powers for the material aid and arms they need, this would be the effective end of nonalignment for many African states.

When racial consideration becomes a serious factor with the African states, militancy becomes the order of march. A few of the more pragmatic states, such as the Francophone Africans, may well stand aloof from direct militant hostility over Zimbabwe, as their historical concerns and political ties are somewhat weaker. Yet, even with them the degree of emotional commitment cannot be gauged adequately. In voting at the United Nations their record on racial issues is similar to that of the English-speaking African states. Even Liberia and Ethiopia cannot resist the pull of the African system on this issue.

Under these circumstances, the revolutionaries will be tempted to return to the old Nkrumah pattern of sponsoring the so-called "true revolutionaries" throughout Africa that almost wrecked the OAU in the early 1960's. Clashes between rival liberation movements would also intensify. Western powers would be under much stronger pressures for intervention in certain areas, on behalf of parties and movements friendly to them. Thus, if only a few African states break the pattern of nonalignment, they can set in motion forces able to break down the system altogether.

In this respect the subordinate white subsystem of southern Africa presents the greatest threat to the Black nonaligned subsystem. The two systems cannot coexist on the same continent, one or the other must change radically. The prospect is for growing conflict between them from the guerrilla actions of the forests to the debates of the Security Council. The Western world does not wish to choose sides but events may force us to decide for one or the other.

6 Southern African Liberation Movements: The Turn to Violence

The end of the comparatively peaceful decade of the African national revolution can be dated from 1964, when Zambia became independent. Since that time, liberation movements have entered a new phase of violence. These tactics have required different methods of organization, new ideologies, and diverse patterns of association and external support.

The turn to violence has raised very serious questions for nonalignment patterns in unliberated Africa as well as the rest of Africa. Earlier nationalist movements which had won independence under less revolutionary conditions preserved relationships with previous metropolitan areas that are almost impossible to preserve in southern Africa today.

Revolutionaries need arms and support from the outside if they are ultimately to win their struggle. This aid requires allies and these external allies invariably exact a price. Under such circumstances, the external great powers are inclined to escalate their intervention on both sides, thereby directly threatening nonalignment.

Liberation movements are highly dependent upon the African nonalignment system and are, in one sense, the beachheads for the extension of that system southward. The conflict with the white Western subsystem of the South, as noted earlier, gives the African system a unity of purpose and policy and in this way strengthens it. Success at any level gives nonalignment added prestige.

On the other hand, frustration and failure create grave dangers for the nonalignment system. This is a highly emotional issue-area for the liberation movements and their supporting African states. Quarrels between rival factions in the liberation parties and differences over the proper sources of external support are highly explosive issues. This is the politics of blood and the winner takes all, for ideology is super-charged. Compromise and restraint are difficult to practice. Therefore, the forces of disunity are as great as those of unity.

The protracted conflict has created a polarization between white settlers and Africans. Oliver Tambo, the president of the African National Congress (South African), in exile, pointed out this change in addressing a rally in London: "For fifty years Africans have fought oppression. Peaceful methods have been met with violence. Now the turning point has come. The African has picked up the gun he laid down fifty years ago."[1]

One of the earlier prophets of revolutionary violence, Frantz Fanon, whose works have become an ideological Bible in southern Africa, has spoken of turning "the absurd and the impossible inside out" and called for the hurling of "a continent against the last ramparts of colonial power." In reference to his own Algerian struggle, Fanon said, "We need only march and charge. We have mobilized furious cohorts, loving our combat, eager to work; we have Africa with us."[2]

Southern African leaders have evoked the spirit of Fanon in their own struggle. While their victory may take several times as long to achieve as the seven-year Algerian war, they are persuaded that their bloody battles will one day be crowned with the same prize. The cost will be great in sacrifice and human lives, but they no longer hesitate to ask this commitment of their people. And they are increasingly embittered against those aspects of Western policies that reinforce the white supremacist system and make the task more difficult and costly. Whether or not the observer agrees with this view, or considers it to be realistic, its possible effect must be considered carefully.

Their nonalignment policies create a dilemma for Africa's liberation leaders. On the one hand, they realize they must have help from the outside to succeed. On the other, they are wary of the tendency of those who supply the weapons and funds for insurrectionary movements to exact commitments and to gain influence. Thus, they are caught in a vise between needing assistance and not wishing to pay for it by mortgaging their independence. Their dedication to the principle of nonalignment within the African subsystem is real; but they are pulled in contradictory directions.

The difficulties of maintaining a nonalignment position are compounded by the nature of the Africans' struggle. Because of the military character of their struggle, their requirements for outside assistance are much greater than those of the earlier nationalist movements, and, they have found to date only one sure source of assistance — the communist world. The West has given little more than sympathy, and very little of that, officially. As a matter of practical politics, liberationists have been forced to regard the Western powers as important sources of support for their enemies. Leaders such as the late FRELIMO president (Mozambique movement), Eduardo Mondlane, are not unaware of the dilemma this creates. Mondlane argued that FRELIMO is neither pro-East nor pro-West, but is pro-Mozambican. However, he continued, "If the West has decided, for reasons of expediency, that it cannot part company with fascist Portugal, and to leave the Africans of southern Africa to fend for themselves, remember it's not our choice, it's yours. We will accept that. But don't be surprised later if we are not very friendly to you."[3] Mondlane was one of the more Westernized African liberation leaders, though by no means a "patsy of Western interests" as his rivals charged. Most other liberation leaders have expressed their frustrations and rage at Western policies in far stronger terms. The assassination of Mondlane in February 1969 eliminated one of the last of the more Westernized liberation leaders.

The writing is clearly on the wall for anyone ready to read it. The leaders of Africa's liberation movements are being forced to diverge from the established pattern of nonalignment more and more. In most cases, they are not Communists, but maintain a broad belief in African socialism. Yet, by virtue of the conditions under which they must fight, they are forced to form alliances with the communist and revolutionary powers ready to help them.

The Liberation Movements

Two basic types of liberation movements exist. The first is the mass movement. The most advanced of these movements have liberated part of their own territory. The second type of liberation movement, elitist groups, usually have split off from the mass movements for ideological, ethnic, or tactical reasons. They have little backing and, for the most part, are ineffectual and divisive.

Usually, the mass liberation movements are older and mobilized more completely, with substantial sources of external support. The more successful movements operate from a sanctuary. In this sanctuary, they train and equip their followers for combat. Refugees infiltrate across the border in large numbers, and the younger men are the major pool of recruits for the guerrilla bands. These movements, moreover, govern certain territory in their colonial areas, where they collect taxes, carry out education and welfare programs, and raise crops as well as train and recruit for combat. Widespread sympathy and support for these liberation movements exists among the indigenous populations of their home territories.

Generally, the elitist type of liberation movement has not developed the strength to carry out significant insurgency operations. Usually, attempts are abortive because the populace is unsupportive politically. At times, elitist groups appear to expend more energy attacking each other than in organizing the insurrection in their own countries.

One of the most difficult problems for liberation movements has been divisiveness. In some areas, half a dozen groups rival each other for supporters and external assistance. The reasons for these differences arise from a complex of factors such as tribalism, personal ambitions, ideology, and differences over tactics. To some extent, the sources of support as well as historical accident appear to enter into their antagonisms. This has been a most serious problem, highly confusing and exacerbating to the African states who have sought to help them.

The Portuguese Territories

Since the FLN defeated the French in Algeria, the best examples of mass liberation movements have emerged in the Portuguese territories. The most successful has been the revolt in Guinea-Bissau.

The Partido Africano da Independencia da Guinea e Cabo Verde (PAIGC), led by Amilcar Cabral, controls a third of the heavily forested countryside of this small Portuguese enclave between Guinea and Gambia. The first congress of the PAIGC was held inside Portuguese Guinea in February 1964, though it had been founded in 1956. One ingredient of success, according to French analyst Gérard Chaliand, is careful preparation of the minds of the peasantry prior to the actual initiation of insurrection.[4] In this way, the PAIGC received massive peasant protection from the counter-insurgency tactics of the Portuguese.[5] In 1969, the Portuguese still held the major towns but were restricted increasingly in their ability to control the countryside. In 1965, an OAU mission was able to visit the liberated areas and returned to report enthusiastically about the success of Cabral's movement. A member of that mission told this writer that he felt the PAIGC was the only recipient of the funds from the OAU Liberation Committee that could demonstrate substantial results.

Most observers agree that the only reason the Portuguese continue to cling to their enclave positions in Guinea is their fear that to let Guinea go would begin a chain reaction throughout their territories in Africa. Thus, they continue to sacrifice their young men on the altar of an increasingly apparent lost cause.

Two smaller elitist parties rival the PAIGC but have not begun any significant action in the field. The Frente para a Libertacao e Independencia da Guine Portugesa, known as FLING, is critical of the Marxist tone of the PAIGC and of Sékou Touré's influence. Their leader, Pinto-Bull, and a small trade union group in Senegal have some support from the tribal and political interests of Senegal that oppose those of Guinea.[6] However, the Senegalese government does not officially take sides. Outside aid has come primarily from Guinea and the OAU. Since most of Guinea's arms are communist in origin, the Portuguese have been able to play up the role of communism in the PAIGC, not without some effect in conservative Western circles.[7]

The other two major mass movements of liberation in Portuguese Africa are Frente da libertacao da Mocambique (FRELIMO) and Governo Revolucionario de Angola no Exilio — Frente Naçional de Libertaçao de Angola (GRAE-FNLA). Each of these major movements has several rivals of varying importance that are ideological and tribal splinter groups.

The longest and most bitter conflict against Portugal has been fought by Holden Roberto's liberation movement, now constituted as a government-in-exile. Operation by what was then the UPA (later GRAE) began in early 1961 and spread most rapidly among the northern tribes, especially the Bakongo. The fortunes of war flowed back and forth, for Roberto was somewhat dependent upon the support he obtained from the rapidly changing Congo governments. During the Adoula period, and later under Mobutu, the Congo (Kinshasa) gave considerable direct support as well as sanctuary to the GRAE training camps.[8] Under Tshombe's government, with its sensitivity to European influences, this help was withdrawn and the GRAE operations were nearly suspended. Deep splits arose in the liberation leadership partially as a result of this external influence.

The GRAE has had a series of perilous conflicts with rival organizations, several of which have been funded and supported by foreign governments, both African and non-African.[9] It was able to establish its initial primacy through recognition by the OAU in 1963 and the Congo (Kinshasa) as the only official liberation movement in Angola. In 1968 its major rival, the MPLA, received OAU endorsement and support. Led by Mario de Andrade, the MPLA consists mainly of predominantly mulatto and Mbundu intelligentsia from the Luanda-Catete region. Their chief difference from the GRAE, other than unwillingness to accept Roberto's leadership, has been their strong ethnic support from the Kimbundu peoples of the north, and their Marxist class-consciousness. They have thereby found favor with the more radical ideological governments of Africa, and have also received OAU assistance. At the end of 1966 they had opened a new front in the eastern Congo, although they were having difficulties with the Zambian government because they disrupted ore shipments by rail through Portuguese territory.[10]

In Angola, the Portuguese periodically have reestablished control over areas they have lost, but they are weakening gradually, while the pressures of the liberation forces have intensified over the years. There is little prospect of a settlement for the near future. However long it takes, and whatever the price, the liberationists have vowed to continue, and the African states give every indication that they will continue to grant the support that makes this possible. The Portuguese also appear willing to make unlimited sacrifices for a long time ahead.

Mozambique is the latest front opened by anti-Portuguese African liberation movements. Dr. Eduardo Mondlane founded the party in 1962 and built it into the major mass movement in Mozambique. FRELIMO claims to have liberated the two northern districts of Niasa and Cabo Delgado, where over 800,000 people live. They also maintain that two-thirds of their training takes place in Mozambique. Tanzania is their major base of operations, with the head office in Dar-es-Salaam. Uria Simango, one of two vice presidents, succeeded on an acting basis to the presidency after Mondlane's death. He is regarded as more pro-Peking than Mondlane though still a neutralist.

The only rivals of FRELIMO are elitist, as the movement has not suffered the same ethnic and ideological fragmentation as the Angolan GRAE. Paulo Guamane, who worked among Mozambicans in South Africa, emerged as the leader of a coalition of dissident elements entitled Comite Revolucionario de Moçambique (COREMO). The major difference has been over tactics. COREMO claimed that the FRELIMO leaders had exposed the people to retaliation before they had developed a capacity to defend themselves. But Mondlane was convinced he had prepared the people well, through extensive education campaigns. Renewed attempts to bring the two groups together after Mondlane's death have failed.

Mondlane was the son of a chief in southern Mozambique. He was educated in South Africa, Portugal, and America and held a Ph.D. in anthropology from Northwestern University. He had a firm grasp of international diplomacy and power structures and did not appear to have been rendered inept for revolutionary leadership by his academic background. Like many of his fellow well-educated liberation leaders in Portuguese territories, he threw in his lot with the peasantry and maintained the critical threshold had been passed, from initial uprising to "prolonged revolt."[11]

The Portuguese are now fighting on three fronts in their African territories. Portugal is a small country, with little industry or surplus funds to spend in years of protracted colonial conflict. By expending half her national budget on her colonial wars, many observers believed her resources would have been exhausted long ago. However, the help Portugal gets as a member of NATO and the interest that international capital and mining concerns have in maintaining Portuguese presence in Africa have sustained her. It should be remembered also that South Africa thinks it has a stake in maintaining a buffer zone between itself and the black African states to the North.[12] Even if Portugal should lose her Western power patronage, she might well become a client of South Africa and solidify further her role in the southern subordinate system.

Therefore, despite the optimistic press statements of liberation leaders, the struggle in Portuguese territories is apt to be protracted. Even the loss of Portuguese Guinea probably would not start an immediate chain reaction, as South Africa may well buttress the colonies for a time. In the words of President Nyerere, the liberation leaders are not despairing too much, but "are settling down to a prolonged revolt." They are stepping up the training of cadres and the supply of arms from the communist world.

Zimbabwe

Zimbabwe is the name chosen by the liberation parties of Rhodesia for their future homeland under African rule. This, and their opposition to UDI, is as far as the agreement has gone between the two rival mass liberation movements discussed previously in Chapter 5, ZANU and ZAPU. Both were permitted a brief period of growth inside Rhodesia and then banned as the settlers felt increasingly threatened. This enabled them to put down roots which UDI and government oppression have not destroyed.

ZAPU has the longest historical role in Rhodesian nationalism and, at the time it was banned, had the widest popular support among the African population. Originally, ZANU split off from ZAPU in mid-1963, under the leadership of the Rev. Ndabaningi Sithole. The basic reason for the split was probably tribal, although both sides deny this. However, the leadership of ZAPU is drawn overwhelmingly from the Matabele tribe, and the leadership of ZANU is mostly Mashona in origin. Since the Matabele constitute 80 percent of the African population, the popular appeal of ZAPU is as much tribal as political. Nathan Shamuyarira, a ZANU leader, has argued that ZANU wanted to create its base operation within Rhodesia, while depending upon outside support. But

Sithole gave greater priority to "the fight from without."[13] If this was a major point of difference at the start, the banning of both movements and the imprisonment of Sithole, Nkomo, and other leaders soon eradicated it.

The OAU has sought constantly but unsuccessfully to bring the two movements together. Unable to choose between them, the OAU simply has supported both. In some cases, individual African nations have chosen favorites: Tanzania and Zambia favor ZAPU, while Sithole and ZANU generally find support in more conservative circles. However, there is no real discrimination against ZANU in Zambia or Tanzania, where it maintains representatives; ZANU broadcasts regularly into Rhodesia from Zambia and has used Zambian soil for staging guerrilla operations into Rhodesia.

To date, neither ZANU nor ZAPU has been very successful militarily. They both have bands of guerrillas which operate in Rhodesia. On occasion, these have engaged in sharp action with the Rhodesian militia and South African security forces. The liberation press reports these as major victories for the Zimbabwe African National Liberation Army. For example, *Zimbabwe News*, August 19, 1967, pp. 3-4, reports two such engagements with losses to the enemy of eighteen troops in one case and fourteen in the other. The accuracy of these reports is questionable, as are the accounts of the Rhodesian government's "wiping out" all guerrilla bands who cross the frontier. Evidence indicates that internal insurrection is growing in Rhodesia, though estimates of its effect vary widely.[14]

Since the "Chimurenga Freedom Fighters," as ZANU and ZAPU are called, have not succeeded in liberating any major areas so far, probably the people do not dare to support them in the direct ways the FRELIMO forces have enjoyed. This is due in large measure to the efficiency of the Rhodesian police and army, who have not hesitated to arrest and detain any African suspected of sympathy for the Chimurenga.

A new direction in the struggle emerged when ZAPU combined forces with the South African ANC. Reports of an extended clash of these groups against combined Rhodesian — South African forces received wide attention in August 1967. In commenting on this engagement, Joe Matthews, a leader of the ANC, indicated that this cooperation arose from a mutual interest in the liberation of southern Africa. He pointed out that the intention was not primarily engagement with the Smith forces, but the infiltrators were primarily "armed propagandists" in the Cuban mold.[15] New tactics and better training began to produce results in 1969. Reports indicated large groups were operating successfully within Rhodesia and the Rhodesian forces have been reenforced by South African contingents.

Even the liberation leaders agree that they are far from their goal. Zambia is not free to give them outright support, because both the United Kingdom and Rhodesia put a great deal of pressure on Kaunda's government. As long as Zambia is vulnerable to these economic and military pressures, she must play a dual role. Thus, Zambia's program of disengaging her economy from Rhodesia and Mozambique is a major factor in the ultimate strength of the liberation movements throughout southern Africa. The Tanzania-Zambia rail link is in many ways the key to Zambian independence. Herein lies much of the reason why the Western world did not support this economically feasible proposition and the task has been undertaken by the Chinese whose motives are not limited to economics.

South Africa

South Africa is the strongest and most important inner citadel of white supremacy in Africa. Highly skilled in the art of counter-insurgency, and in the totalitarian control of a subject majority, the South African government has virtually destroyed the internal organizational structure of the major nationalist movements. The mass movements of the African National Congress of South Africa and the Pan-Africanist Congress of South Africa have had their major leaders jailed by the South African government. The secondary leadership has thus gone into exile, where they operate from offices in Europe and other African states.

For a time, small underground movements such as POQO and Spear of the Nation were effective. But even these were dismantled eventually with the help of a network of informers the South African police have built. Colin Legum has concluded "no effective sabotage has occurred inside the Republic since the resistance movement was broken in 1962." [16] However, opposition continues in various sectors of the Transkei, especially Pondoland (that could be very important to the guerrilla movements in the future).

The next phase is the gradual increase in power and infiltration of "armed propagandists" across the borders. Both the PAC and the ANC are training men for this task in various African and communist countries. This task is very difficult under present circumstances. The Botswana government has made its position clear. It does not intend to be a staging ground for guerrilla units. It is too dependent upon South Africa. Prime Minister Seretse Khama indicated that they try to police the situation themselves and do not inform South Africa "when we have captured terrorists nor do we make any reports of their movements to South Africa." [17]

Rivalry between the two mass movements, PAC and ANC, is very intense. Virtually no coordination, even of infiltration, takes place. Despite the urgings of the OAU and the other benefactors of the liberation movements, the leaders will not consolidate. The reasons go back to the time when they had real tactical differences, the ANC being the leading nonviolent organization and the PAC emerging in reaction to the failure of the nonviolent policy. Since that time, vested interests appear to have developed. In exile organizations, this splintering usually results from the frustrations and rivalries of leaders whose livelihood depends upon their dexterity in exercising control. Also, the influence of rival powers and ideological groups who try to use these organizations for their own purposes is of major importance.

One of the most effective guerrilla campaigns was conducted by the South West African Peoples Organization, (SWAPO) which, over a period of years, has succeeded in infiltrating the remote areas of Ovamboland where there is very little white influence. However, the long supply lines from Zambia through Botswana, southern Angola, and the Caprivi strip were very difficult to maintain. South African reaction was severe and resulted in the trials of alleged South West African "terrorists" and collaborators in the Supreme Court of Pretoria in late 1967. This trial took place despite world opinion that South Africa no longer has jurisdiction over South West Africa. The South African government subjected the accused to long imprisonment without trial and *ex post facto* conviction under the Terrorism Act of 1967.

Liberation leaders no longer look for an early triumph. They have adopted a long-term strategy built upon a step-by-step conquest from the Portuguese territories to Rhodesia and then to South Africa.

External Aid

Their own dedication would not carry the exiled liberation leaders very far. They are highly dependent upon sympathy and support from the Pan-African world and among opponents of racism elsewhere in the world. This support has taken the form of OAU grants-in-aid, training programs, funds and education facilities for leaders and students, arms and guerrilla equipment, provided particularly by Algeria and Tanzania. In return for this, the liberation leaders have become embroiled in the alignments and counter-alignments of external politics.

The OAU has been the primary source of direct funds; and despite the complexity of liberation politics, OAU members support this program strongly. Thus, the percentage of the OAU budget designated for the Liberation Committee has increased, although the total amount has not substantially increased since the total budget of the OAU has declined. At the 1967 Kinshasa meeting of the heads of state, $2 million of the $3.1 million budget went to "freedom fighter" support. The meeting also decided to establish a military aid committee to coordinate the activity of various African states in this area.[18] The amounts of aid designated to various groups is classified. Estimates place the total for groups like GRAE and the ANC at about 20 percent of the budget.[19] Not all African governments contribute to this fund, although they often use this as an excuse for not extending aid themselves. Non-African governments can contribute through this fund, as Yugoslavia has done. President Nyerere served for several years as Chairman of the OAU Liberation Committee, an onerous job, as his major task was to arbitrate between rival liberation movements.

These rivalries have presented numerous opportunities for African states to play politics and revolution with each other. Nkrumah never trusted the OAU Committee, and preferred to operate through his own Bureau of African Affairs. Through this program, he maintained a shadowy, CIA-type of operation across

Africa, frequently utilizing exiled leaders to intrigue against other independent African states. Nkrumah was not the only one to play this game. To have a number of revolutionary leaders dependent upon them was a matter of prestige for certain African states. Guinea, Algeria, and the UAR have been the most active in this matter. The effect upon the liberation movements has been to intensify splits and hostilities. Also, this Pan-African political maneuvering has created certain alignments among the liberation movements and with outside Great Powers.

Alignment Pressures

For the most part, Western governments have shunned direct association with liberation movements, but the Communist powers have not hesitated to move into Southern liberation politics. A number of private Western associations have assisted various educational and training programs, but these are humanitarian rather than military.[a] The International Legal Aid and Defence Fund is one example. Funds from this organization go to the legal defense costs of political trials, and to the relief of the families involved.[20] George Houser, of the American Committee on Africa, reporting on his visit with several liberation leaders, said, "The Western countries themselves are just not considered a significant influence in the politics of liberation movements."[21]

Liberation leaders are fully aware of these limits and have turned to the communist world for the military and other support they cannot get from African states or the West. Communist countries ship arms through Cairo or Dar-es-Salaam in substantial and growing amounts.

Alignment and Nonalignment

Despite this growing dependence of the liberation movements on communist sources as the military phase is stepped up, communism has not taken over, either ideologically or in terms of influence. Yet, the trend cannot be ignored.

A certain alignment is evolving among some liberation movements that does not reflect ideology, internal organizational structure, or the extent of success, as much as the source of external aid, both from African states and from Communist powers. FRELIMO, MPLA, ANC, SWAPO, ZAPU and PAIGC form one grouping. This group gets assistance from Eastern European countries, and not any significant amount from China. The second group, PAC COREMO, SWANU, GRAE and ZANU are supported more from Peking than Moscow. Egypt, therefore, has become an important conduit for the first group, while the second utilizes Tanzania as a base. Ironically, when the United States has chosen to play favorites, it has usually supported those receiving support primarily from the Chinese, rather than from the Russians.

This emphasizes the irrelevance of United States strategy in Southern Africa.

[a]Private foundations and churches have contributed to the Mozambique Institute of FRELIMO located in Tanzania.

In the long run, this can only deepen the influence of both the Russians and the Chinese. The danger, then, is that a conservative American government may panic and decide to enter the game on the side of the "non-Communist" white racist system. Any cursory reading of the liberationist press shows that they are virtually convinced that this has happened already, through extensive United States military aid to Portugal and through Western investments in South Africa.[23]

Conclusion

Thus, an alignment pattern appears to be forming in Southern Africa that differs from the nonalignment patterns that emerged from earlier nationalist victories in North-Central, East, and West Africa. The regimes of southern Africa cannot be toppled except by major, forceful, and extended revolutionary activity, which cannot be achieved without substantial assistance from outside the African continent. If the Russians and the Chinese supply this source of aid, they will exact a certain price. Since World War II, Western states, and especially the United States, have intervened directly in Asia, Africa, the Middle East, and Latin America to prevent the extension of communist power and influence.

A confrontation on the Vietnam model, with clear racial dimensions, seems inevitable in southern Africa, unless at least two developments take place: extensive unofficial support for the revolutionary movements from Western non-governmental organizations and a disengagement of United States financial power from supporting the subordinate Western system of southern Africa. These developments would mean acceptance of the revolutionary African governments that replace white supremacy, even if they include certain communist elements. The frenzied fear of any and all forms of communism has made it difficult for the United States to play one communist group against another, and has virtually disqualified America from exerting any influence in liberation politics. Nonalignment still operates among liberation groups in Southern Africa, but its chances of survival over the next decade are slim indeed.

Moreover, the impact of these trends upon the pattern of nonalignment in the rest of Africa has been felt already. The more revolutionary governments are committed to maintain pressure on southern African regimes. Even moderate pro-Western governments must answer to a highly race-conscious constituency, and must appear to be militant, although privately not extremist. The initial impact appears to have strengthened the race issue-area character of the nonalignment system. However, if intervention from the Western world should escalate behind the white regimes, it could create explosive forces under the prevailing pattern and set the radicals against the moderates in a concerted pattern of alliance and counter-alliance.

7 The Community and the Commonwealth: Toward New Patterns

A most important consideration for nonalignment is relations with the former colonial powers. Even though a state may become officially independent and elect its own president, the dependency relationship may not have been transformed, in fact, into something else that can be called nonalignment. All kinds of direct and indirect cultural, economic, and political involvements continue for most states after independence. The former metropolitan power can take back with the left hand what it has given with the right. A systems approach has demonstrated clearly how these informal relationships can be more important than the formal ones. Therefore, the constitutional form of an association, like the Commonwealth of Nations, tells us very little unless we know the efficacy of this system in the eyes of its constituent states and the nature of their commitments and benefits.

In coming to any conclusion about the true character of the new relationship, we should recall the meaning of nonalignment. In its pure sense, it is a state of independence among new nations in which decisions of foreign policy are primarily internal and self-determining, as opposed to control from without.

With the fragmentation of the Western and communist blocs, nonalignment must now be seen in terms of a multipolar world and the relationship of African states to both former colonial powers and new world powers.

The issue of independence has been particularly important for former British and French territories because these two powers have sought not only to maintain many existing relationships with the independent states but also to give them institutional form through a British Commonwealth and a French Community. Thus, a certain conflict has arisen between the stated ideal of nonalignment and the reality of a continuing relationship, formalized in institutions that in many ways have the characteristics of alliances with great powers.

The issue really concerns the substance of these relationships. One view is that the Africans have accepted subordinate relationships.[1] Others argue that each is a free community in which each member retains full control of its decision-making processes and "is a free association between peoples and not in any way a rigid alliance."[2] The answer is not simple or academic as is shown by the extensive discussion and debate on this issue. The dilemma has been pointed out by William Zartman: "The desire to solve problems, which often exceeds system capabilities and requires outside help, clashed with the desire to maintain the autonomy of the system."[3] He refers especially to Tanganyika's call, in 1964, to Great Britain to restrain mutinous armed forces. In this case, clearly, the system was incapable of self-regulation, and outside force was called upon.

Crucial to the analysis is the difference between subordinate and autonomous systems. Michael Brecher described five distinguishing characteristics, of which the most important was that "changes in the dominant system should have a greater effect on the subordinate system than the reverse."[4] Thus, the fall of the de Gaulle government would have a greater effect on the French Community than any change in the governments of the African members of that Community. This description is not really satisfactory because changes in the government of any great power might have a similar effect on small African states. In fact, this is the essential character of the relation between great and small powers. The crucial component of subordination is, as it has always been under colonialism or other forms of subordination, lack of self-determination. Thus, subordination is the absence of a viable and measurable degree of autonomy related to foriegn policy determinations. Clearly, membership in a subordinate system would be contradictory to nonalignment.

Of course, what was true about an international system yesterday may no longer be the case. Whether membership in the British Commonwealth or the French Community is incompatible with nonalignment depends upon an assessment of the evolving character of these two systems.

Commonwealth and Community

The French would be the last to admit that the British Commonwealth of Nations had served as a model for their own Community in any way. However, the evolution of the Community since 1960 has been toward the free association of independent nations, bound together by a community of economic, cultural, and political interests, that has characterized the British Commonwealth of Nations from the beginning of this century.

The transformation of many new, non-Western and nonwhite states from colonial status has caused substantial change in the character of the French and British colonies. The British Commonwealth was able to make the transition more easily since it had established earlier autonomous relations with Canada, New Zealand, and Australia. The French, however, had to move from a tightly controlled relationship in which these overseas territories were regarded as "an integral part of France."

Yet, in the postwar period, the British Commonwealth, too, had to find a form that would give greater autonomy to the new nations. This was found in the substitution of a President of the state for the traditional British

Governor-General, who had represented the British Crown as legal head of state. In this way, the United Kingdom, in this wider postwar Commonwealth, simply became the first among equals at Commonwealth meetings. (Although the Queen of England is, in British eyes, the Head of the Commonwealth, her actual status with the non-Western members is highly ambiguous.) As in the United Nations General Assembly, the United Kingdom has only one vote, the same as Sierra Leone and Gambia. Usually, meetings are held in England with the British Prime Minister as host. Thus, a thin legal veil has been drawn over the actual anchor position of the United Kingdom in the association of Commonwealth of Nations.

Not all former British territories have opted to remain within the Commonwealth. The Arab states of Africa, particularly Egypt and the Sudan, have severed this relationship, although the Sudan remained within the sterling zone and continued close diplomatic and cultural ties until the Rhodesian UDI and the Middle East crisis of 1967. Egypt's earlier rejection influenced the Sudanese to opt out as well. However, all the black African, English-speaking states elected to remain within the Commonwealth. The United Kingdom urged this relationship upon them and frequently, as in the case of Kenya, acceptance of this role hastened independence.

The mantle of Commonwealth status has rested rather uneasily on the shoulders of several of the more revolutionary leaders, though they all favored the system at the outset. Nkrumah's views of the Commonwealth, during the early years of his rule, were that: "It is the only organized world-wide association of people in which race, religion, nationality, and culture are all transcended by a common sense of fellowship. No policies are imposed on it from above. It does not even seek unity of policy. . . . This is not a bloc. It is not a power grouping. It is a club or a family of friends who see their continuing friendship as a strand of peace in a troubled world."[5]

The Prime Minister of England could not have expressed the purpose of the system with more sentiment. From this perspective, the Commonwealth was not theoretically in conflict with nonalignment. Later, when Nkrumah dismissed his British Chief-of-Staff for complicity in an intrigue against his government and accused the British press of trying to overthrow him,[6] he was reflecting the doubts that increased as internal dissension grew. This suspicion regarding policies that were inimical to the Commonwealth was mutual, as some British observers felt Nkrumah's autocratic system was contrary to the Commonwealth spirit as defined in 1926 in the phrase "free institutions are the life-blood of the Commonwealth."[7] Although Nkrumah withdrew recognition of the United Kingdom in late 1965, in compliance with the OAU resolution on Rhodesian UDI, Ghana did not leave the Commonwealth. But diplomatic nonrecognition clearly creates problems because the Queen of England is the official head of the Commonwealth.[8]

The possibility that certain African states would become alienated and withdraw from the Commonwealth was very real. This, as Denis Austin noted, might arise from the triumph of a left-wing government and hostilities against the United Kingdom for complicity with South Africa.[9] However, "between the Commonwealth African countries and Britain there are innumerable ties of association which, though they may be affected from time to time by quarrels at government level, are able to weather the storms . . . because of the advantage to be gained from maintaining them."[10]

Tanzania's relations with the Commonwealth reflect this alienation and uncertainty. Tanzania has not withdrawn officially, yet Nyerere has not participated in several important meetings, such as the Commonwealth Defense Conference in London, during the summer of 1966. President Nyerere stated he would not have signed the final communique of the Conference because of differences over dealing with the Smith government.[11]

The ambiguity of the role of states who do not have diplomatic relations with the United Kingdom illustrates the rapidly changing nature of the Commonwealth. While the political aspects of the system have been weakened, economic and financial ties have often been the strongest bonds. These have been changing rapidly, too, particularly in the light of the increased importance of African trade with the EEC.

Francophone States and the Community

The French Community has been one of the most rapidly evolving international institutions — indeed, it has evolved almost out of existence. Originally, the Community was formed by de Gaulle as an attempt to hold the Francophone states of Africa in close relation to France. Simultaneously, France was moving toward closer association with Western Europe in the EEC. Both France and the African states, primarily for economic reasons, have given primacy to the EEC association over the Community.

However, the evolving relationship has had strains and problems. The Francophone states are divided between the moderates and the radicals, as are the former British territories. From the start, there has been hostility and opposition to what have been regarded as the neo-assimilationist aspirations of France, expressed through the Community. And considerable dissatisfaction has arisen from the terms of association with the EEC that reflected the earlier, weaker bargaining position of the African Francophone states.

The original plan of the Community, as conceived in the 1958 French Constitution, did not provide independence for the overseas territories, but gave them internal autonomy, and linked them to France in foreign affairs, finance, defense, trade, higher education, justice, and tele-communications through a consultative Executive Council and a Senate, presided over by the French President, who was elected by all citizens of the Community. However, France retained control through the representation system of the Executive Council and Senate. An Arbitration Court completed the structure.[12] This arrangement won strong support among the more conservative African leanders, such as Houphouet-Boigny of the Ivory Coast. But the more revolutionary, led by Sékou

Touré, saw it only as a device to retain subordination of the African states. In a shrewd and open-handed manner, France permitted the African territories (in the 1958 Referendum) to decide whether they would accept the Community or not. Only Touré's Guinea chose immediate independence. France acted decisively against Guinea, withdrawing personnel and support, thus isolating the center of opposition to the concept.

More moderate African leaders, such as Léopold Senghor of Senegal, Modibo Keita of Mali, Sylvanus Olympio of Togo, and Anmadou Ahidjo of Cameroun, were determined to work for independence without paying the price of economic separation from France. They were assisted in this goal by the intransigence of French policy over Algeria, which made her vulnerable to the attacks of independent African states. In 1960 the former French Trust territories Togo and Cameroun, under the auspices of the United Nations, obtained independence while remaining within the broader French system. In June 1960 de Gaulle yielded to the pressures and amended the Constitution to permit members of the Community to choose independence.[13] All the African states elected this option quickly as it enabled them to retain the benefits of the Community without sacrificing direct sovereignty.

This meant the Community had become, in the phrase of Senghor, a "Commonwealth à la française." However, only a few of the African states that had left the Community bothered to rejoin (Central African Republic, Chad, Congo Brazzaville, Gabon, Senegal, Malagasy). As with so many international associations, the substance of relationships became much more important than the form. All the African states, inside and outside the Community (with the exception of Guinea and Mali), continued intact the preexisting ties with France: financial, aid, trade, and military.

Despite the failure of the Community in form, France has been able to evolve a much closer relationship with the Francophone African states than exists among the Commonwealth states. It has been so close, in fact, that African leaders outside the French system frequently have accused the African states within it of neo-colonial dependency.[14] In the early phases of the system's development, the charge that sovereignty was only a shadowy form among the Francophone African states was largely valid. They have continued to evolve, however, and this characterization may not be correct since 1965. The two galaxies of the Community and the Commonwealth may be approaching each other very rapidly in substance as well as form.

Economic Integration and Independence

The primary issue for most of the independent African states in their relations with Europe has been development. A few of the more revolutionary, like Ghana under Nkrumah and Guinea, have placed ideology first, and have rejected, by assumption, any program that appeared to compromise their independence. Guinea broke with France entirely in order to assert this position; but Ghana maintained diplomatic and economic ties with the United Kingdom until near the end of Nkrumah's reign. After his overthrow, diplomatic ties were soon restored. Economic diversification of aid and trade was never as critical for former British colonies as for those of France. Most leading British territories had highly diverse trade and aid programs with other powers by the time they achieved independence.[15] Shortly after Ghana had become independent, the United States had become her largest customer for cocoa. At the time of Nigerian independence, many nations other than Great Britain were granting economic assistance.

The principal economic benefit to the former British states in the Commonwealth was participation in the sterling area, with its financial underpinning of currency loans and limited aid. Low preferential tariffs were of some benefit, especially as the EEC restrictions consolidated against the nonassociated states. A considerable amount of British technical and professional skills were easily accessible and closely linked to their developing educational and vocational programs.

However, the African Commonwealth states became less dependent upon these sources as opportunities for diversified trade grew, and other great powers made attractive offers of aid. These non-associated states wanted to find a basis of cooperation with the EEC; and in 1965 Nigeria established an agreement for associated status that set the pattern for a whole new trend.

Nigeria's movement toward the EEC indicated that many English-speaking African states were prepared to set aside their fears of political assimilation by France and Europe. It also provided an example of the autonomous bargaining power of fully independent African states, in eliciting a more favorable agreement from developed Western European nations.

The basic agreement initiating the association of the African territories of the Western countries, France, Belgium and Italy, was the Treaty of Rome. Signed in 1957, prior to the independence of any of the territories concerned, the agreement did not modify the subservient economic status of the colonial territories. The African territories were brought into the European Common Market and thereby enjoyed a wider market than France, through a complicated reduction of tariffs. However, they in turn provided reciprocity for European manufactured goods, by phased reduction of restrictions.[16]

The big issue was whether African states could diversify and industrialize under these conditions. A substantial EEC Development Fund was established as the sweetener, and endowed originally with $581.25 million for the first five years.[17]

Economists and political leaders have disagreed vigorously over the value of the benefits derived by the former territories. English-speaking Africans and economists are far more skeptical of the long-term benefits than their Francophone counterparts.[18] Unquestionably, sectors of the economy and certain elites benefited from the subsidies and generous aid terms of the development fund. Whether long-term balanced growth in the interests of the developing countries (along the lines of the UNCTAD principles) took place in the first five years is very questionable. Nevertheless, most of the political elites were satisfied with the arrangement, and eighteen states renewed the agreement for five years at Yaounde in 1964 with what might be called moderate improvements in their position *vis-à-vis* the EEC. Further favorable reductions of tariffs on semi-processed goods were obtained, and the development fund was increased to $800 million, with a strong emphasis on economic, social, and technical assistance. Also, a new category of loan aid was made available.

In 1969, this extension expires and the African states, strengthened by the accession to association of Mali and Nigeria, under different terms, will be in a position to demand much more from Europe. The Nigerian agreement set a very important precedent in that it limited reciprocity in terms of Nigeria's own interests and Nigeria remained out of the development fund. Therefore, she was free to make her own deals for aid and to diversify these throughout the world. Kenya, Uganda, Malawi, and Tanzania have begun negotiations for similar association; the Nigerian arrangment has convinced most African states that they can gain much economically from penetrating the European markets and the political price will not be their independence or nonalignment.[19]

This is abetted by the growing economic independence of several of the Francophone states. Mali, in particular, has demonstrated the flexibility of the system. Despite her strong connections with China and Russia, she negotiated herself back into the franc zone, in 1968, in order to gain French support for a currency that had become nearly worthless. The bargain was hard, though, with the French requiring many administrative and budgetary reforms.[20] Niger, Senegal, Gabon, and Congo Brazzaville have been the most active in building diversified trade outside of the EEC. Yet, some Francophone states have maintained ninety percent of their trade patterns with Europe. As a group, the rate of diversification among the Francophone states has been far slower than among the British-speaking states. This explains a great deal about political policies, as a close reciprocal relationship between politics and trade tends to exist.

Yet, trends toward diversification seem inevitable and the Africans are coming together on this basis, regardless of their colonial backgrounds. Obviously, it is much too early for an African common market, because their economies, as Senghor pointed out, are competitive rather than complementary. This is not changing very rapidly. Regional economic integration (such as the East African Common Market or UDEAC in Central Africa) has achieved minor success. Diversification and industrialization will promote regional African trade. African economies must move in this direction to free themselves not only from their former colonial masters, but also from the financial and economic power of more developed countries. Thus, weak African economies can only approximate the goal of economic independence at this point, though they are able to move toward it individually and collectively.

Eur-Africa is an outmoded imperialist dream, but close relationships with Europe, as with the EEC, are by no means contradictory to development, diversification, and autonomy. Certainly, the developed agrarian countries of the

Commonwealth, such as New Zealand and Australia, have demonstrated how autonomy can exist within a close relationship. However, this analogy must not be carried too far, as other ties of culture and race distinguish the Western Commonwealth from the non-Western Commonwealth.

Military Ties

Security links are an important indication of the nature of a nation's status. Initially, African security forces were created, trained, and equipped by colonial powers, and in some cases Western military bases were maintained in the African states after independence.

These relationships have changed rapidly as the metropolitan powers have been disengaging their participation and control over military units. However, the ties of tradition and training are strong; the subtle influence of former colonial powers remains, though operating through new forms. The most striking examples of this influence have been the requests by African governments to the former colonial powers for help to put down mutinous army forces. Since the last of these requests in 1964, both sides have been very reluctant to resort to these means of keeping a pro-Western regime in power.

British military links have dissolved more rapidly than the others. After the abortive Nigerian Defense Pact and the difficult debate that ensued, the United Kingdom has not attempted to preserve its position with independent African states in any formal way.[21] The use of this issue by the Opposition in Nigeria to create Anti-British as well as anti-government feeling, indicated the dangers of such a policy. Moreover, since their departure from Suez in 1956, the British have not felt that any part of Africa, except South Africa, was important to them as a military base. The 1968 decision of the Wilson government to withdraw British forces east of Suez by 1971 further lessened the security ties of the United Kingdom on the African continent.

The exact nature of the British government's commitment to utilize its forces to put down an insurrection in an African state is highly relative to the circumstances of the revolt and the policy of the current British government. British forces were used at the request of the East African governments in Tanzania and Uganda in 1964 to put down mutinous army elements. The intervention of British marines clearly saved the Nyerere government in Tanzania. Given the withdrawal of England from Aden and the changed relations with Tanzania, this type of action is most unlikely to recur. A similar action, which did not go quite so far, took place on behalf of the Kenyatta government in Kenya in 1965. British marines were said to be prepared to land if the expected coup of Vice President Oginga Odinga's forces had taken place.[22]

This type of intervention has become less likely despite the United Kingdom's interest in preserving certain friendly governments and protecting British nationals. Moreover, coups have become a hallmark of African systems, and an unfriendly government may be replaced easily by a friendly one tomorrow, and vice versa. From the African point of view, to preserve one's power by virtue of direct great-power intervention is an immense loss of prestige and authority. The one condition that might precipitate such intervention is the clear linkage of a communist power to a coup. While the British are less inclined than the United States to react to this type of revolt, they are not immune to the anti communist virus. However, their natural caution in such a situation is reinforced by their diminishing capacity to become involved.

The major continuing source of British military influence in Africa is through training and, to a lesser extent, providing equipment. At the time of independence, all the African armies still maintained a contingent of British officers who were seconded to them from Her Majesty's Imperial Forces. In 1967, the United Kingdom earmarked £ 1.3 million to cover half the cost of British military personnel loaned to African states. There were 880 of these people serving in Ghana, Kenya, Zambia, Malawi, Sierra Leone, Sudan and Libya.[23] The continuing training programs for officers from these African states at Sandhurst and other military academies in England have been just as important. Very few African countries, Ghana being the first, have established their own military training academies.

Grants-in-aid and loans have enabled a number of the African states to purchase military equipment. Kenya and Ghana have modernized their navies, and Zambia has strengthened her forces with the help of United Kingdom sources. Nigerian arms support was reinstated in 1967, despite the Civil War, after the Russians supplied MIG fighters to the federal government.

In English-speaking Africa the trend has generally been toward diversification, as countries move away from their independence dates and gain greater financial independence. Other powers have made more attractive training and arms aid offers, and the disposition is to accept at least some of these in order to maintain a balance or to receive other types of favors, such as aid agreements, that frequently are packaged with arms deals in the insidious game of modern diplomacy. Ghana, Tanzania, and the Sudan, ideologically nonaligned, have been the quickest to introduce diversification and thereby to "decolonize" more rapidly the role of the former metropolitan power in their military affairs.

The military component of the French Community system has been much more important and persistent than in the Commonwealth. The French have more consciously maintained a military policy and presence in Africa than have the British. This was due, at least initially, to their deep commitments in the Algerian war.

At the time of independence, the French had a published military assistance program with each of the new states, except Mali and Guinea, for the supply and standardization of weapons. Training in France, or under French officers, was a prime part of the agreement. France specifically required that other aid sources could not be used unless France agreed. Madagascar, Senegal, Cameroun, and the Ivory Coast have been the primary recipients of this military aid. This has made these countries militarily dependent upon France — a condition that has not altered very much since independence; Germany has begun, however, to send some assistance to a few states of the Francophone group.[24] France has gradually reduced the number of bases and troops maintained in Africa. However, all the armies of former French Africa, except Guinea, still use French officers for training purposes.

France also has an elite mobile paratroop division ready for immediate action anywhere in Africa. The famous 1964 French intervention in Gabon on behalf of the deposed government of Leon Mba, who had been overthrown by an army-inspired plot, continues to arouse suspicions of French "neocolonialism." The French will not respond, however, to every call for help. This was demonstrated by their refusal to aid Abbé Fulbert Youlou's government in Congo-Brazzaville. The criteria that govern French intervention are not entirely clear because the Abbé was a close supporter of France and was replaced by an increasingly radical government, indicating that the French may not always associate their interests with pro-French conservatives. France's distress with the military coups in Upper Volta and Central African Republic, which abolished austerity measures in favor of increases in civil servants' salaries, suggests that their attitudes are determined in part by considerations of efficiency and honesty in African governments.

France probably would aid the regimes of Presidents Senghor and Houphouet-Boigny if they were threatened, but might not help the regimes in Gabon, Upper Volta, Chad, and Niger.[25]

This French interventionary pattern is changing, as is Great Britain's. The African governments are becoming more independent financially; a number of countries, such as Congo-Brazzaville, Mauritania, and Mali, have opened military ties with the Communist powers. After de Gaulle's departure, the personal ties of certain leaders were reduced greatly. As *Le Monde* put it, "If politically minded soldiers are part of the French tradition, so is revolution."[26]

The French politics of military aid in the Francophone countries have encountered surprisingly little political resistance. Except for Guinea, they have talked far less about neocolonial military manipulations than have English-speaking African countries, with much of the criticism directed against Americans. The exclusion of the United States from most former French areas may result largely from the compliant African public attitude. In general, de Gaulle's policies were the most popular in French-speaking Africa, and those of the United States the least popular. No doubt the British have suffered from guilt by association with the United States.

Politics of Diplomacy

All newly-independent African states who have arrived at this status primarily by peaceful means have had a strong tendency to associate themselves rather closely with the diplomatic objectives of the former metropolitan power, not only because of the economic and military ties noted previously, but also because of cultural and even ideological identity. The almost solid Francophone African support for French policies, initially over Algeria, and on the major issues at the United Nations, was not simply "neocolonial manipulation." This support resulted at least in part from the genuine affinity that the new bourgeois African elite had for French culture and government and, therefore, the French view of the world.

This attitude, however, has changed very rapidly, as have other factors in the French and British systems. By the time of the Stanleyville Drop, Mr. C.D. Ganao, representative of Congo-Brazzaville at the United Nations and one of the most outspoken critics, could say, "What is to become of the black part of mankind, assuming that you admit that it actually exists?"

The fragmentation of the English-speaking states into what might be called pro-British and uncommitted states took place more rapidly than in the francophone states.[a] Yet the general trend for polarization into a pro-French and an uncommited group has continued among the original eighteen Francophone states of the OCAM.

During the first two years of their independence, both Ghana and Tanzania followed British leadership on a number of international issues very closely. The case of Ghana's backing of the United Kingdom and the West over the Hungarian crisis of 1956 is one example. Tanzania supported the moderate African position in the first Congo crisis, but Nyerere's sympathy for the political heirs of Lumumba, under Gizenga, became important during the second crisis.

Generalizations about trends are a bit dangerous, as the case of Ghana suggests. After the coup against Nkrumah, Ghana became one of the staunchest diplomatic friends that the United Kingdom has in Africa. However, the disposition of most English-speaking African states to become more critical politically of the former metropolitan power continued, as generally reflected in greater independence of policy and voting behavior. Such a trend is not always perceivable, and changes in leadership may reverse it. It is nonetheless one of the most definite patterns in the nonalignment spectrum.

The above generalization does not mean that all the pragmatic, Westernized African states will become revolutionary, and therefore nonaligned ideologically. Such a development is related to a host of internal factors that are not considered fully here. If statements of presidents and voting patterns at the OAU and at the United Nations are considered the major indicators of diplomatic independence, the majority of the English-speaking states are becoming more independent of the United Kingdom. They are not, then, the client states of the United Kingdom, as Nkrumah frequently suggested, nor the neocolonial stooges of Western imperialism, in the communist parlance. Comparisons to American relationships with Latin American countries are tempting and, to some extent, meaningful, but the relationship is different in political as well as economic ways.

The diplomatic politics of French-speaking African states has followed a similar pattern, but more slowly and in a more involved manner. Except for Guinea and Mali, the Francophone states of West and Central Africa, plus Malagasy, followed a rather uniform pattern of diplomacy from the formation of

[a]The term "anti-British" does not reflect the basic attitude of even Nkrumah's government.

the Brazzaville group to the establishment of the Union of Africa and Malagasy (UAM) in 1963. The two primary leaders were Senghor and Houphouet-Boigny. Though differing in style, these two elder statesmen set a moderate, pro-French, pragmatic direction. They were embarrassed by France's Algerian policy, but enthusiastic about the benefits of association with the EEC. Houphouet-Boigny, who served in the Cabinet at one time, received many honors from France. The president of Senegal, Leopold Senghor, has been for many years a leading intellectual Francophile. His political philosophy is based upon the "personalist" principles of the French Catholic Left,[27] and his ideas of "Negritude," while African in inspiration, are not racist or anti-Western, but continue the humanist universalism characteristic of African socialism. The French-oriented concepts of these two men set the tone of policy for the early years of independence.

A divergence between ideologies began early in 1965. Houphouet-Boigny is basically a political conservative and a Francophile, for whom Eur-africa is not anathema, but a desirable relationship. Senghor, on the other hand, is a genuine intellectual and proponent of an independent African political thought, culture, and social organization. The political manifestation of these differences clashed over the impatience of the Ivory Coast with the limited role of the OAMCE, which had been created as an economic and technical integrating agency. Houphouet-Boigny and several other pro-Western leaders, such as Maurice Yameogo of Upper Volta, wanted a more political organization of the Francophone states that would include the ex-Belgian territories as well. France and other interested Western powers probably favored this objective.

Much of the motivation for the formation of the Organization Commune Africaine at Malgache (OCAM) was the reaction to the Stanleyville Drop. The West received support only from Nigeria and some of the Francophone states. The revolutionary states gained a number of new allies as a result of the differences within the OAU over the issue (see chapter 4), and the influence of Nkrumah and Touré seemed to be ascendant. As one Western observer put it, "The aggressive ex-Casablanca states . . . had arrogated to themselves the right to speak for all of Africa at the United Nations, and at international conferences. . . . The moderates were now determined to make their voices heard."[28]

One of the first actions of the core states of OCAM, the Entente, was to lead the campaign against Ghana, which was the center of subversive activities against their governments. This action culminated in the abortive campaign to block the holding of the OAU conference of the heads of state in Accra in October 1965. President Senghor had been drawn into the original denunciation of Ghana's subversive activities, but Touré and Keita persuaded him not to oppose the holding of the Accra conference. The OCAM then took up other matters, such as holding the line against the growing influence of Communist China in Africa, gaining diplomatic support for Moise Tshombe's government in the Congo, and mounting a propaganda war with Guinea.

By mid-1965, a growing number of French-speaking states had become disenchanted with the political orientation of OCAM. The first to break from the organization was Mauritania, whose President, Ould Daddah, despite his reason to be grateful to those who had first championed his state and made him acting president of OCAM, was opposed to the admission of the Congo under Tshombe. Undoubtedly, the reason for this disagreement was Mauritania's proximity to the North African states, especially Algeria, which were bitter foes of Tshombe. The fact that this was not simply a North African versus black African issue was confirmed by the statement of President Ahidjo of the Cameroun, who declared, "We did not attend the Abidjan Conference because we did not agree with the admission of the Congo-Leopoldville to the organization."[29] As would be expected, Congo-Brazzaville under the "scientific socialist" government of Massemba-Debat and Pascal Lissouba supported this criticism of the OCAM. The latter had developed strong ties with China, as had Mali, and was not about to give them up under pressure.

Originally this division in OCAM did not include Senegal and Chad. However, by the end of 1967, it was clear that Francophone Africa's character was radically changing. The deposition of Tshombe in the Congo and the strong and independent leadership provided by General Mobutu indicated that a powerful new force had been added. There were now three camps: the radicals and their allies: Guinea, Mali, Congo-Brazzaville, Cameroun, Burundi, Mauritania and Chad; the moderates: Senegal, Congo-Kinshasa, Central African Republic, Rwanda, and Togo; the conservatives: Ivory Coast, Upper Volta, Dahomey, Niger, and Malagasy.

Curiously, this division has nothing to do with membership in the French Community. This is further evidence that the Community is a meaningless organization today in terms of French relations with Africa. The most important French relationship is with the more conservative and moderate Francophone states. The emerging role of the Congo-Kinshasa within this group will loosen further their direct ties to France, as the Congo is oriented toward Belgium and is influenced considerably by the financial role of the United States.

The political-diplomatic ties of the Commonwealth and Community nations have thus weakened as these African states have moved into the midstream of international relations. There are no French nor British blocs of African nations. Some African states such as the Ivory Coast and Malawi have, for various reasons, retained closer ties than many of the others. Ten years after the first independent African states began to emerge, the most important ties with Europe are with the international systems known as the British Commonwealth and the French Community.

Nonalignment and Europe

The answer to whether Africa has a community or subordinate system relationship with Europe is that, in general, Africa is moving toward more developed nonalignment. The Commonwealth and the Community that the British and French created out of the former colonial pattern has slowed but not deflected this direction.

This does not mean that special relationships do not have great importance. The association with EEC has been so valuable that it will be continued and extended to encompass most of the independent states. The same is true of the functional benefits of the Commonwealth to its African members. Yet, this relationship will favor the African states increasingly as they develop strength and diversify their contacts with world power, thereby improving their bargaining position.

African states view membership in any international system largely in terms of the benefits and leverage they can get from it. The Community and the Commonwealth are not only sources of substantial technical and financial aid but also give the small African states leverage among great powers they would not have otherwise. Frequently the English-speaking Africans have used the Commonwealth to pressure the British government, especially on southern African issues. Probably, the United States never would have undertaken the sanctions campaign against Rhodesia were it not for its concern over relations with independent African states. Similarly, French accommodation with the Algerian radicals was greatly influenced by Francophone African attitudes.

Yet the movement toward greater autonomy within these associations is most pronounced. This movement may be slowed down for a time, especially if the United States continues to reduce its aid programs in Africa. The United States has been an important support for maximizing the benefits of bargaining by the new leaders. To a lesser extent, this has been true of alternatives offered by the Communist powers also. Armed with these alternatives and their own growing self-assurance, the African states have begun to ask much more from Europe in return for what they give. Their increasing ability to make collective demands has strengthened this position greatly.

The dilemmas of economic autonomy and political self-rule have not been resolved. Yet, some interpreters, reacting against the excessive optimism of the great dawn of freedom in the early sixties, have concluded with unwarranted pessimism that Africa has no choice but to accept the terms of European economic direction for the indefinite future. This conclusion greatly oversimplifies the actual situation.

Africa has had and still has subordinate states, but, outside Southern Africa, it does not have subordinate systems today. This situation creates a climate highly conducive to African nonalignment policies. The United Kingdom and France have come to accept nonalignment in principle. Certainly they differ in their interpretation of its content. All great powers (including France and the United Kingdom) are assimilationist by virtue of their power. They continue to regard Africa as their prime sphere of interest outside Europe, and they resist the attempts of rival powers to encroach on their traditional domain. However, their methods of resisting are far more flexible and sophisticated than they were in the nineteenth century. They have learned to live with the contraction of their power in relation both to the United States and the Soviet Union and to the small states of Africa. The concept of nonalignment is quite compatible with the special relationship they have sought to maintain.

Moreover, France and Great Britain benefit from nonalignment, for it fends off the increasing pressures of the super powers to create alignment systems in Africa. The United States and the Soviet Union present the real challenges to African nonalignment policies. The Community and the Commonwealth, as they are developing currently, are no alignment systems.

Eur-Africa is as impractical as the restoration of the Holy Roman Empire. Those who dream of it exaggerate the degree of cultural affinity that exists and the economic advantages to be gained from such a system. The long-term pressures favor a nonalignment subsystem, which is by no means incompatible with economic and diplomatic cooperation between great and small powers. A very practical example of this was the Franco-Algerian oil agreement in 1965. This treaty between two states provided for the cooperative exploitation of the rich oil deposits of the Sahara. Algeria gave up nationalization in favor of a "mixed economy" with a much larger percentage of the returns. France gave up higher profits for a special relationship. An Algerian official summarized their feelings: "The oil agreements, by putting an end to the prerogatives of the oil companies, vestiges of colonialism, open a new era not only in Franco-Algerian relations, but in the future evolution of all the 'third world'."[30]

Some Americans are amazed that the United States is less popular with the emerging nations than the former colonial powers. Much of the explanation lies in the lessons that the former colonizers have learned and in their ability to accept the limits that even constrain the policies of great powers.

The long-term subordinate economic relationship between Africa and the external powers is in terms of development and trade. Statistics indicate this relationship is becoming less favorable for African states. In this respect, African states find their autonomy to be drastically limited. They have few choices and little bargaining power. The choice between the trading terms offered by the developed West or by developed communist states is not very wide in many cases, despite the opportunities created by nonalignment.

This inequitable relationship remains the basic problem of development for the African states. Until the new nations can strengthen their trade and investment position, they are highly vulnerable to political pressures. Nonalignment is thus a form of protection against these pressures, though it does not provide a final equitable settlement. This can come only as a result of a major shift of great power policy toward the UNCTAD principles of equity.

8

Nonaligned Black Africa and Communist Powers: Bridge or Battleground?

The opening of diplomatic relations with communist powers (including China) has been an important indicator in the development of nonaligned policies. A major motivation has been a desire to benefit from the diversification of contacts: trade, aid, and cultural exchange. Since the communist powers are an important new source of such assistance, the nonaligned nations have entered into a vast variety of relations with them. The most important question is how this relationship with communist powers, like the Soviet Union and China, has affected these new and rather weak African states, in terms of their development and the nonaligned system.

Frequently, spokesmen for Western powers have expressed the view that this relationship was not only lacking in any really tangible benefits for their former wards but also was highly dangerous to their newly found independence. The Africans have usually replied that the Western powers are blinded by a desire to preserve their own interests and that Africans have no intention of exchanging "one form of imperialism for another."

Are the Africans simply näive, or are the Western powers incapable of objectivity on this matter? One point is clear at the outset — the diversification of African relations with the communist powers has many aspects; no such thing as a \communist world or a Western world exists any longer. In fact, the rivalry between China and the Soviet Union is in many ways more important than the old cold war division. Thus, the relationship must be examined in terms of the different policies of the states involved, and the varied types of programs.

Communist Theory and Nonalignment

Much in the doctrine of communism suggests that communist states are opposed inherently to the basic concepts of nonalignment. The Marxist view of the world proclaims the inevitable sweep of the revolution through all non-socialist political systems. Anything not communist is capitalistic or feudalist and must be taken over by the forces of "scientific socialism." Then, all socialist systems will join hands in a final war against capitalism. Lenin, in his book, *Imperialism, the Highest Stage of Capitalism,* outlined his conclusions regarding the inevitable role of the colonial world in this revolutionary victory of the proletariat over imperialism.[1]

However, since Lenin's time, communist doctrine toward "national democratic" regimes has undergone many modifications. These changes relate to the character of the national bourgeoisie, the democratic fronts, and their policies toward outside powers. Differences between the Russians and the Chinese on these matters affect assumptions as well as tactics. The uniform Communist attitude toward nonalignment has yielded to rival communist views and policies.

The Soviet Union

At the height of the cold war, many observers concluded that the Soviet Union could not recognize and respect the independence of nonaligned nations. This interpretation was supported by the statements of the Soviet leaders up through the Stalin era.

After Stalin's death, this view changed and they were able to view the African nationalists with greater objectivity. But Communists, even scholars, had great difficulty in freeing themselves from the ideological predilections that distorted their view of political movements in Africa.[2] For example, the Soviet scholars first regarded the CCP of Ghana as a "conservative bourgeois movement". Later, they reversed their position, as they had over Ghandi in India and other Asian nationalist movements which they then termed "progressive" governments worthy of Soviet support.[3]

The attitude of the Soviet Union to nonaligned African states is related closely to the changes in Soviet theory. Since de-Stalinization, they have evolved a policy of supporting the new anti-imperialist class they call the "national bourgeoisie." This class is deemed sufficiently progressive to stage a national revolution and inaugurate the processes of change. Not all the emerging nations have been awarded the classification of national democracies, but those that have been placed in this category, like Indonesia, India, the UAR, and Ghana, became special recipients of support from the Soviet Union. The tendency for the national bourgeoisie to slip back into feudalism or association with the imperialist powers was to be opposed strictly. Various tactics were justified in the anti-imperialist struggle, even employing traditional ethnic sentiments.[4] If the national bourgeoisie falls under the sway of Western neo-colonialism, the progressive elements are to fight reaction by revolution.

Thus, the key to Soviet support or opposition became, in the post-Stalin era, the interpretation of whether a particular regime was "national democracy." A natural tendency to favor the burgeoning single-party systems of Africa developed, although distinctions were made between progressive and feudal types. A. Lerumo, writing in the *World Marxist Review*, argued that all single-party systems could not be called progressive, since Senegal, for one, was "neo-colonialist." However, single parties that are "united fronts of national liberation" are "meeting the challenge of neo-colonialism and imperialism."[5] In practice, the definition of a national democratic government turned upon its willingness to enter into significant contacts with the "socialist zone."

This led to a generally favorable view toward the nonalignment policies of the new African states. As Mikhail Kremnyev argued: "The emergence on the world arena of these independent states . . . is changing the world balance of forces." He continued, "The nonaligned countries standing for friendly cooperation among all states on an equal footing, are making a contribution to the solution of the major international problems. . . . Nonalignment is the alternative to a pro-imperialist foreign policy, and is again only compared to the latter."[6]

Two significant developments led to a broad tactical interpretation of what constituted a national democratic state. The first was Communist China's serious entry into African politics as a rival revolutionary force to the Soviet Union. The second was a series of reverses in the fortunes of several of the regimes considered most progressive and, therefore, favorable to the Soviet Union — particularly Ben Bella's government in Algeria and Nkrumah's in Ghana. The collapse of the Stanleyville governments under Gizenga and Gbenye, successively, was another. Although they attributed the overthrow of these governments to intrigues by the United States, the effect was not to intensify Soviet counter-revolutionary theory. Rather surprisingly, the Russians became more pragmatic and shifted their emphasis from political revolution to modernization and development. Despite their propaganda line of blaming the imperialists, they appeared to understand that incompetence and corruption had much to do with the collapse of the regimes of their protegés. Therefore, they broadened, rather than narrowed, their interpretation of the types of governments they could support.

In the light of this, it is not surprising that the Soviet Union, from the Khrushchev era on, has viewed nonalignment in Africa with a favorable eye. It feels that the emergence of these new states from Western colonialism helps alter the world balance of forces. Moreover, in major international problems these new states opposed militarism and imperialism. Since nonalignment "bears a distinctly anti-imperialist character and is in substance one of the forms of the anti-imperialist struggle," it is to be supported. However, it is not the preferred status; "the recommended type of international relations is that being moulded by the socialist system. . . ."[7]

The Soviets rationalized this stand by regarding them as "pre-capitalist regimes" that would move toward the left as the national bourgeoisie became stronger. Even the Ivory Coast was viewed this way. "It seems that no independent African government, however stalwartly pro-capitalist, need be dismissed as too unlikely a candidate for Soviet favours."[8] This belief was a remarkable change from earlier dogmatism. Thus, in practice, the way was cleared for broadly-based Soviet support of nonaligned African states.

Chinese Theory

China is the latest great power to develop important relations with new African states and liberation movements. Her intervention has affected considerably the policies of the Soviet Union and the United States and has given nonalignment diplomacy an entirely new dimension. The Chinese Communists appear to have been motivated by two major considerations: 1) advancing their national brand of communism, *vis-à-vis* the Soviet Union, and 2) finding allies and resources in "the struggle agains United States imperialism."

Africa has become a major area of contention in the worldwide communist debate over Marxist theory and revolutionary tactics. The Chinese have sought to demonstrate, by the African example, that the Russians have become the tools of the imperialists through their "revisionism." Their major quarrel with the Russians began over the issue of whether communism can coexist with capitalism. Mao Tse-tung attempted to repudiate Khrushchev's famous opposition, outlined in 1956 at the 20th Congress of the Communist Party of the Soviet Union, that coexistence with nuclear-armed capitalist states may be necessary for an indefinite time.[9] This was the major objective of China at the Afro-Asian Solidarity Conference at Cairo in 1957, three years before the final Sino-Soviet split.

In theory, the Chinese have little patience with the Russian concepts of the progressive "national bourgeoisie" and the "national democratic" regimes. They maintain that African societies are "ripe for revolution," and that this long period of transition the Russians see is only a mirage of capitalist propaganda. As in the revolution in China, the Chinese believe that the peasantry can be a revolutionary force, replacing the Leninist reliance on an industrial proletariat. Therefore, they believe that the African peasantry, whose revolutionary consciousness has been developed by oppression and Western racism, should be encouraged to use the Chinese model for revolt. In their view, the national bourgeoisie are usually lackeys of neo-colonialism, and in most cases their regimes should be undermined by liberation forces of the "uninterrupted revolution."[10]

It would be fair to characterize Chinese policy as aimed at turning Africa into a battleground for war against the United States and the Soviet Union rather than to support nonaligned African states as a buffer zone in the cold war or a bridge of transition toward "scientific socialism." However, recognition of nonalignment as the theoretical basis of Chinese policy[11] was implied in the eight points on foreign aid Premier Chou En-lai stressed during his 1964 tour of ten African countries. In practice, however, they have generally followed the rule of recognizing as nonaligned those countries most ready to deal with them. Theoretical concepts have been used primarily to combat Russian influence and extend their own.

However, in implementing this principle the Chinese have differed significantly from the Soviets. The Chinese thrust in the new African states has been on racial identification and political propaganda among those opposition groups and minority elements most ready to listen. An examination of the respective aid programs shows an important difference in type, as well as quantity. While the Chinese stress political persuasion, in limited areas, the Russians give far greater emphasis to technical and economic programs, widely spread among moderate and radical governments.

Communist Tactics and Programs

Both of the great communist powers have been interested in building communist ideology and organizations in Africa. Their approaches have been different, but at least they have shared this goal. However, their escalating rivalry has done more to slow down their progress than any internal conditions in the new African states.

A standard method of organization used by the Communists has been the "People's Front" operation, that has either a liberation, trade union, or cultural public purpose. One of the most important has been the Afro-Asian Peoples Solidarity Organization (AAPSO), which was begun by Asian Communists and then, through Cairo, extended into Africa. From the beginning, it claimed to be the vehicle for continuing the "spirit of Bandung." This was never really true, because the Soviet Union was not a Bandung power and many of the African and Asian countries that had been at Bandung had little or no official association with AAPSO. From its inception, this organization was a curious mixture of official and unofficial entities. Most of the African groups were either liberation groups from non-independent territories, or exiled opposition elements, such as the ANC of South Africa, or parties in independent countries, such as the UPC of the Cameroons. Their motives in cooperating were primarily monetary rather than ideological, as they hoped to gain some additional leverage with the help of the Communist powers in AAPSO.

At first, the Soviet Union was the dominant communist power in the AAPSO. At the Cairo Conference of 1957, only the Guinea delegation supported China. However, the Chinese took quick exception to the Soviet claims to be an Asian power and muscled their way into the inner sanctums of the organization. Their principal coup was the establishment of the Solidarity Fund of the AAPSO, with an office in Conakry. This became the primary source of the AAPSO funds for African liberation movements with Ismael Touré as Chairman and with the Chinese, not the Russians, on the steering committee.

After that, maneuvering between the two communist powers characterized the meetings of the AAPSO from Moshi in 1963 to the abortive Algiers Conference in 1965. Despite the overthrow of Ben Bella (who was to host the Algiers Conference), the Conference might have been held if the Russians had not realized that the Chinese had the upper hand and, therefore, pressed for its postponement.

Pro-Chinese groups have developed primarily within the liberation movements (see previous chapter) among Congo (Kinshasa) exiles, and in Mali, Zanzibar, Guinea, Congo-Brazzaville, and the Communist Party of the Sudan. On the trade union field, Nkrumah-sponsored AATUF, whose African affiliates broke with the ICFTU, has not fared well since the Osagyefo's overthrow. Its demise has allowed the radical trade unions to come more directly under the communist source of funds based in Eastern Europe. Also, the Soviet-sponsored World Peace Council has been a major vehicle for Russian penetration. This Council has held a number of conferences and organizations in African states, such as the World Without the Bomb Conference in Ghana in 1962. The Soviet Union has exploited these to attack Western policies and enhance its own reputation.

Only in very few instances are independent, Communist-controlled organizations or publications permitted to exist in the African states. The Sudan, where the Railway Workers and Gezira peasant organizations have long been under communist control, is an exception. Pro-Peking and pro-Moscow factions contend with each other constantly within the single-party organizations of the African states. Powerful personalities, who generally are not Communists themselves, use these contending factions for their own political purposes, as did the former Vice-President of Kenya, Oginga Odinga, and the once powerful Tawia Adamafio in Nkrumah's Ghana.

Occasionally, "African Communist" intellectuals have gained positions of great influence within party structures, such as Ismael Touré in Guinea, and Kai Batusa (an editor), and Sam Ikoku (a Nigerian exile) of the Kwame Nkrumah Ideological Institute. Such men have been of tremendous value in the penetration of party machinery and government positions. During the last year of Nkrumah's rule, the party bookshops of the CPP carried communist literature, particularly Chinese,[a] almost exclusively. However, the communists have not created powerful controlling centers of influence within party organizations anywhere in Africa, either through direct or indirect means, with the possible exception of the Bureau of African Affairs in Ghana under Nkrumah.[b] Press reports in the West generally have vastly overrated the organized character of this influence. Even during the growth of the Stanleyville secession in the Congo, the actual influence and control of the Chinese over the insurgent groups was marginal.

The communist powers have been more successful in influencing significant governmental programs through official aid programs. The most outstanding cases are related to security. Nkrumah requested that the Soviet Union train his own security guard, and at the time he was overthrown, he had created an independent security force led by Russians and Cubans. Thus far, no other African leader has attempted to follow this example. Chinese military aid to Congo-Brazzaville and to Tanzania has been extensive, and at one point the Chinese had a liaison officer to every command in the new Congo (B) army.

Chinese training activity has been strong on the island of Zanzibar, but, as of 1968, the balance of similar Western-trained technicians on the mainland was maintained.

[a]This was noted by the author during a visit to Ghana in late 1965.

[b]The Bureau was the primary source of scientific-socialist thought and Soviet propaganda. Though it would be wrong to assert that all the major figures were Communist (e.g., A.K. Banda), they were certainly oriented to the East.

Arms Aid

Russia has been far ahead of China in military aid programs; not only do the Russians have greater resources, but also they are less hindered by ideological reservations. Thus, they have been able to penetrate important countries like Nigeria. They supplied planes and Czech pilots to the Nigerian government when the Nigerians were unable to obtain assistance from the West during a critical period of the Biafran secession. Their activities in the Moslem world, especially Egypt and Algeria, have been extensive.[12] In 1967, the Russians concluded a £ 40 million arms agreement with the Sudan.

Major shipments of Chinese arms have gone to East African ports. Most of this material finds its way through the government of Tanzania into liberation movements. China supplied the Algerians with large amounts of arms during their war with France.

Communist troops have not intervened directly in Africa, although this possibility should not be excluded. The Egyptians were prepared to call for Soviet volunteers during the Suez crisis of 1956, and Lumumba asked for such help at one point, but later withdrew his request at the insistence of Nkrumah. The Biafrans appealed to Mao for help in 1968 with no result. Thus, Communist military intervention remains a threat rather than a reality for African nonalignment and for world peace.

Many pragmatic states, such as Kenya and Nigeria, have acquired communist arms, but the policy of diversified military aid has been pursued in the main by the radical, nonaligned countries; Egypt, Algeria, Guinea, Mali, and now the Sudan, all obtain a heavy proportion of their arms from the East. Some depend on the communist world more than on the Western world for arms. This challenges previous patterns, but does not in itself eliminate nonalignment, any more than when these same countries drew primarily from the Western powers. It will be recalled that nonalignment consists of several components in addition to military ties.

Economic Aid

Aid from the communist powers has many purposes, including expanding trade as well as winning favor in world politics. Both China and Russia have used aid programs to extend their trade agreements with the African states, frequently on a barter basis; they will take sisal, coffee, or sugar in exchange for machinery or bicycles for Africa.

Often the Soviet Union has been willing to undertake large-scale and long-term programs, such as the Aswan Dam on the Nile and the proposed dam at Buri in Ghana. Such aid carries a low rate of interest, usually two percent. Support for industrial projects has been a major communist program. A number of the Eastern European states, especially industrially advanced Czechoslovakia and Eastern Germany, have cooperated on these. The Chinese, in contrast, have not gone in for spectacular long-term projects, but have concentrated on technical assistance and loan barter agreements. A favorite Chinese device for undermining Soviet aid relations has been to make loans at no interest at all, as in the case of the £ 7 million Ghana loan, and Sino-Tanzanian cooperative schemes. Also, the Chinese have made a great deal of mileage out of requiring their technical personnel to live at the level of their African hosts, though their diplomatic personnel frequently maintain lavish standards.

China has varied from her pattern of moderate loan and aid agreements in the negotiations of the East African Tar-Zam rail link. Even in its survey stage, this is one of the most important communist aid programs in Africa. The cost of the program, according to an official Tanzanian economic survey, will be approximately £ 125 million.[13]

Both China and Russia appear to be interested in shifting the trade pattern of many African states, all of which have traded only with the West previously. Already, they are the predominant trading partners with Mali, Guinea, and the UAR, and they have begun to make inroads in other areas. The trends are sharply upward, as shown in Table 8-1. The Soviet Union rapidly expanded its economic relations with the new African states after 1960, and the Chinese began significant trade and aid programs in Africa about 1966.[14]

Ideological outlook definitely correlates with the extent of relations established with the communist powers. Except for the more radical, they have been unwilling to trade with China, perhaps fearing retaliation from the West. Barriers to relations with the Soviet Union have fallen very rapidly since the fragmentation of the cold war blocs. This has been precipitated by internal and external conflicts of the new African states. The attempted Biafran secession has swung Nigeria toward Eastern Europe, where it can get military assistance This has opened new trade opportunities for the Eastern Europeans, for they have to be paid for their arms. The Sudan took a similar turn because of the anti-Western feeling that arose out of the 1967 Arab-Israeli War. Somalia, in its conflict with Western-backed Ethiopia, has found friends in the East. While the arms flow to Somalia has receded, trade has increased.[15]

Similarly, Tanzania has increased its trade relations with communist powers primarily because of external problems. Nyerere is a leader in the liberation struggle against Portugal, Rhodesia, and South Africa. Tanzania, therefore, has become the primary channel for arms and aid to the liberation movements, whose diplomatic difficulties with the West have blocked certain Western channels. As a result, they have turned rapidly to the East for goods and markets.[c]

Ethiopia has had long-standing economic relations with the Soviet Union despite the conservative character of the Ethiopian government and its close relations with the West. The Russians helped build a $250 million oil refinery at Assab; they have provided fifteen full scholarships to Ethiopians annually for study in Russia; approximately 600 Soviet technicians, including many teachers and medical personnel, were employed in Ethiopia as of 1967. However, Chinese relations are virtually nonexistent.[d] China's aid and trade goes to the Sudan and Somalia, who are involved in border disputes with Ethiopia.

In Black Africa, China has been most successful in Congo-Brazzaville and

[c]Tanzania has begun substantial shipments of sisal to China; 1,500 long tons, worth £100,000 in 1967.

[d]Ethiopia recognizes the Peoples Republic of China, but has no diplomatic relations with it.

100

Table 8-1

Foreign Aid to Africa (in millions of U. S. dollars)

African Exports to:	Trade 1955	% Change	Trade 1958	% Change	Trade 1959	% Change	Trade 1960	% Change	Trade 1961	% Change	Trade 1962	% Change	Trade 1963	% Change	Trade 1964	% Change	Trade 1965
Soviet Union	11.0		107.6		112.2		109.6		195.8		169.1		146.0		..		..
Eastern Europe	96.8		143.1		134.7		147.3		178.9		185.0		200.0		..		..
Total Trade	107.8		250.7		246.9		256.9		374.7		354.1		346.0		360		455
% Change		+243.0		−4.4		+4.0		+45.0		−8.5		−2.3		+0.4		+38.0	

African Imports from:	Trade 1955	% Change	Trade 1958	% Change	Trade 1959	% Change	Trade 1960	% Change	Trade 1961	% Change	Trade 1962	% Change	Trade 1963	% Change	Trade 1964	% Change	Trade 1965
Soviet Union	26.9		143.4		174.8		208.8		152.6		138.0		95.0		..		..
Eastern Europe	80.1		118.4		123.5		135.7		169.7		175.0		182.0		..		..
Total Trade	107.0		261.8		298.3		344.5		322.3		313.0		277.0		440		610
% Change		+250.0		+13.5		−13.4		−6.8		−2.9		−11.5		+70.0		+32.0	

Tanzania. In the former, the Chinese, using Chinese technicians, have undertaken to construct a textile complex. It includes all operations from spinning to manufacturing garments. A substantial part of the cost is covered by an interest-free loan of 600 million CFA francs ($25 million).[16] One of the latest agreements between China and Tanzania involved a joint Chinese-Tanzanian shipping line, at a cost of £ 1.5 million. Tanzania's share of the cost is provided by an interest-free loan from the Chinese and by profits from the company. When completed, the Chinese-built Tan-Zam railway construction project will become a very important means of trade with the East.

The Soviet Union has begun significant trade with Senegal, one of the more conservative Francophone states, through an agreement to provide ten refrigerator ships valued at 882 million CFA ($3.5 million), most of the cost being covered by the 1965 Soviet loan of 20,650 million CFA (about $83 million).

The distinction between Russian and Chinese aid and trade patterns with African states is becoming increasingly blurred. The Chinese have entered the field of large-scale aid programs since 1967 with their commitment to the Tan-Zam rail link. Moreover, they are developing industrial projects. The Soviet Union enjoys much wider relations, but the projection of trends indicates the Chinese may not be slow in catching up, despite their limited resources and industrial capacity. They have determined to enter Africa to demonstrate the mutual advantages of non-Western trade and development, but even more to exploit what they consider to be ripe revolutionary environments.

African Responses

Initially, Africans were suspicious of communist intentions in Africa. Even Ghana took two years to recognize the Soviet Union. Not until 1964 could a major Chinese leader take an extensive tour of Africa. This was due not entirely to the attempts of the Western powers to keep the Communists out. The Africans themselves, even the more revolutionary ones, were suspicious of the intentions of the great communist powers and fearful of the competitive atmosphere that recognition of them would create. By 1968, only thirteen African states had diplomatic relations with the Peoples Republic of China. They were Algeria, Congo (B), Guinea, Kenya, Mali, Mauritania, Morocco, Somalia, Sudan, Tanzania, Uganda, UAR, and Zambia. Except for a few Francophone African states, all had diplomatic relations with the Soviet Union.

Relations between the African states and the communist powers have varied considerably, determined in some cases by the ideological perspective of the government in power. This relationship was changed by a *coup d'état* in Ghana in 1966. After the formation of the Ankrah government, relations were all but severed with China and cooled considerably with the Soviet Union. Many projects and trade agreements were discontinued or revised. However, this did not happen to the same extent in Algeria. After the fall of Ben Bella, the communist powers lost much influence within the government, but externally at least relationships remained much as they had been.

Other than the United States, China has had the most difficulty for it is the country most suspected of carrying on subversive activities. Following a rash of military coups in West African states in 1965 and 1966, both Dahomey and the Central African Republic suspended diplomatic relations with China. This break angered the Chinese. They accused the two African governments of giving in to American pressures, suggesting that "the United States and the Chiang Kai-shek gang" has been responsible for the military coups.[17]

Earlier, the Chinese had encountered similar difficulties in Burundi. With the dissolution of the Nyamoya government and the assassination of Prime Minister Ngendandumwe in Burundi, the large and well-financed Chinese embassy was closed, and a major base for directing operations in the northeastern part of Congo-Leopoldville was lost to China. Jomo Kenyatta in Kenya became increasingly disturbed in 1965 by reports about Chinese subsidies for the rising power of Oginga Odinga. Finally, in March 1965, under the influence of a group of young leaders in the New Kenya group, Kenyatta curbed the flow of Peking funds into centers such as the Lumumba Institute in Nairobi. He also forced Vice President Odinga out of the government and expelled several leading Chinese newsmen and diplomats. Chinese complaints that the American Ambassador, William Attwood, and the CIA were responsible for their difficulties did not impress President Kenyatta.

Conclusions

Some observers have concluded that the Chinese have become disillusioned with their prospect in Africa and have cooled their ardent wooing of Africans. This theory is not substantiated by the growing numbers of Chinese diplomatic and technical personnel flowing into Africa. Reverses in Central Africa have been more than compensated by progress in East and North Africa. East Africa is much more accessible for China by trade routes. Moreover, the Arab world's growing alienation from the West provides an excellent entry point. Once the Tan-Zam rail link and the new Tanzanian Chinese shipping line are under way, China will have improved means of trade and contact. The biggest remaining question is the extent of Chinese resources and the willingness of the Chinese government to make sacrifices for revolutionary promotion in Africa. Probably, the outcome of the struggle for power within China will influence this decision substantially. If the technicians and party professionals finally win out over the old revolutionaries, the scale of Chinese operations in Africa might be reduced.

Russian interest and influence also remains high in Africa. Some observers report a disillusionment and withdrawal, but little evidence supports this conclusion. The emphasis of Russian aid programs has shifted from spectacular industrialization to the support of programs that improve existing agriculture and mining industries. Russian distress over the corruption and ineptitude of

African leadership is similar to Western reactions. Yet, it has not affected the gradual increase and spread of Russian aid. The total amount rose and percentage increases were high. The drastic reductions in American aid are not paralleled in Russian or Chinese programs.

Both Russia and China have suffered major reversals resulting from antagonism aroused by their ideological warfare over communist ideas and movements. Africans are confused and frustrated by the self-defeating contention between the two communist powers. Nothing could be better calculated to defeat the notion of communism as "the wave of the future." The natural distrust Africans have for the intentions of outside powers was strengthened when a conference allegedly called to advance the liberation of Africa was dominated by communist rivalries. This contest, more than the counter pressures of the West, has reduced the role of communist power among the new states.

The rise of communist interest in Africa has, on the whole, promoted the possibility of nonalignment by establishing a real polar power alternative to the West. If communist power had lacked substance, it would have been very difficult for the fragile plant of nonalignment to take root. Certain countries, particularly Guinea and Algeria, found a real alternative to Western aid when they were confronted with the complete suspension of Western assistance. The Western world has not boycotted any African country entirely, as it did Cuba, following the 1959 revolution, though the pressures in that direction have been strong. There is little doubt that Guinea would have become the first Soviet-aligned state in Africa if the United States had joined the French boycott in 1958.

Some African states have been tempted to lean too heavily for their own economic benefit on support from the East. Ghana is an example. The numerous uneconomic industries she established with the help of Eastern European countries and the short-term credit used to import East European consumer goods proved to be disastrous. Except for a few of the revolutionary states, most Africans have not become dependent upon communist aid or trade and have used it as a supplement and, to some extent, a bargaining device with the West.

The communist powers have intervened rarely in internal African affairs. The outstanding cases to date have been the two Congo crises. The more serious was Lumumba's request for Soviet aid and airplanes during the first Congo crisis. This request was rescinded in time, but if such steps had been taken, Western interests probably would have retaliated much more strongly than they did, and the cold war might have flared into a Vietnam-type way in the Congo. This might have caused a lining-up throughout independent Africa that could have destroyed nonalignment for many years. The danger of such a step being taken today has been reduced by a growing awareness, among Africans as well as the communist powers, of the probable consequences. In short, the nonaligned African subsystem has received *de facto* recognition.

Indirect intervention through the support of revolutionary leaders and liberation movements is the pattern of the future for communist influence. As has been discussed in the last chapter, this policy could lead to a gradual alienation of several African states from the West and a drift toward alignment and dependence upon the communist powers. Herein lies the real long-term danger to nonalignment as a working international subsystem in Africa. Bitter racial antagonisms aroused by a struggle over Southern Africa might well induce a large part of Africa to align itself with the communist world.

A decline of communist-power interest and influence in Africa does not seem likely in view of their interests and growing capacities. China may well find that her revolutionary expectations do not materialize and her mood may eventually mellow. But almost inevitably, in the racially explosive and developmentally frustrated atmosphere of Africa, incidents will occur, and China will seek to use strife and revolt against the United States and the West in her unyielding campaign to unite the non-white and underdeveloped world against the "citadel of wealth and imperialism."

9

The United States and Nonaligned Black Africa

Although most of Africa has become a nonaligned subsystem, American policy has never accepted nonalignment fully as a viable, long-term position for African states. Opinion in American policy circles has differed considerably on the issue. Yet despite official American expressions of sympathy that have been issued at various times, particularly under the Kennedy Administration, American policy-makers have not encouraged the nonalignment system as a long-term fixture of the international system. The reasons are complex but, in the main, stem from the postwar alliance system constructed in response to the Cold War.

Now that a nonalignment system has taken root in Africa and the Cold War pattern has changed, a review of this basic policy becomes necessary. Part of the difficulty has been that some United States policy-makers have misunderstood the role of nonalignment. They say that it threatens American interests because its purported independent neutral position actually serves as an entering wedge for communist powers in the Western alliance system.

Although the systemic role of the nonalignment subsystem in the international system as discussed in these pages has little recognition in American policy, there has been a shift away from the earlier theological rejection of neutralism by leaders such as John Foster Dulles and George Meany who condemned it as immoral and Communist-inspired. Since the Kennedy Administration, nonalignment has been condoned as a short-term policy for small powers, provided it conforms to what the United States considers to be legitimate nonalignment. In the parlance of realists, anything is legitimate which does not conflict with American national interests. Apparently, this was the basis of Arnold Rivkin's conclusion, early in the Kennedy era, that "the recent foreign-policy posture of all the self-declared African neutrals in the Congo crisis cannot be meaningfully covered by an acceptable definition of neutrality."[1] President Kennedy's recognition of the legitimacy of nonalignment was qualified by this realism as indicated by his inaugural address:

To those new states whom we welcome to the ranks of the free, we pledge our word that one form of colonial control shall not have passed away merely to be replaced by a far more iron tyranny. We shall not always expect to find them supporting our view. But we shall always hope to find them strongly supporting their own freedom — and to remember that, in the past, those who foolishly sought power by riding the back of the tiger ended up inside.[2]

Thus Kennedy reserved the prerogative of deciding who was "foolishly" trying to ride the tiger in terms of America's interests. This view did not indicate that the United States supported a systemic definition of nonalignment, but only that the United States could accept legitimate independent policies. The limitations of this perspective were revealed in the ambiguities of Kennedy's policy in Southeast Asia. In Africa, where American interests were not under attack so directly, greater flexibility became the basis of American policy under Kennedy and accounts in large part for the continuing popularity of the Kennedy image in Africa. Under Lyndon Johnson the theory of the American position on nonalignment did not change, but practice turned back toward a hard-line view of what conflicted with the American interest. The Kennedy recognition formula was not repudiated specifically, but in practice United States power was employed more directly on behalf of those who were considered to be friendly, and support was gradually removed from those such as Ghana and Guinea whose nonalignment became increasingly "illegitimate." The most dramatic instance of this hard-line interpretation was the American intervention on behalf of Moise Tshombe in the second Congo crisis of 1964.

Under President Johnson the basic proposition of "reward your friends and punish your enemies" flourished. Nonaligned states became suspect if they undertook actions that, in the view of the United States, promoted the extension of communist power in Africa. This view reflected a growing opinion that nonalignment threatened the Western alliance system by weakening the attachment to it of new nations. Therefore, among American policy-makers in the State Department and other agencies, residual distrust of the realism and practical basis of nonalignment persisted with only minor modifications. And beneath the veneer of the United States enthusiasm for the independence of colonial peoples and wary recognition of the nonalignment principle persisted a primordial hostility against all nations who failed to unite in the common cause against those who were, in their view, the obvious enemies of mankind.

In a remarkable way, United States official policy has paralleled that of the Soviet Union whose suspicion also has persisted toward the dependability of the nonaligned when it came to the real interests of Russia. Nonalignment is, after all, a small power system antithetical to the concept of a bipolar world organized around the interests of two great powers.

Analysis of the basis of American policy toward Africa suggests how this highly inflexible, very narrow, and in many respects self-defeating attitude developed. The changes toward greater acceptance and even support of nonalignment that have taken place in Great Britain and France contrast significantly with the basic inflexibility of American policy.

Early Policy

Often the lack of in-depth contact with the African continent has been cited as a primary source of weakness in American relations. This is only partially true as the absence of fixed interests might have been transformed into an asset under more imaginative leadership. Africa was a backwater in American policy consciousness until recently and remains in a secondary priority category despite academic and journalistic discovery of Africa during the past decade.

In comparison to Latin America, Africa has not been an area of large United States investment and trade. The United States stayed out of the late nineteenth-century scramble for Africa despite the interest shown by certain members of the Foreign Service in the Berlin Conference. The United States considered only Liberia to be a preserve of American interests, and this was a very low priority area reflecting the weakness of the Afro-American within American society. In the view of James Coleman, American involvement until the end of World War II can be characterized as an "age of indifference."[3] The United States took slaves from Africa, but gave very little in return. A few missionaries and schools were all that America gave Africa in exchange for the human lives and labor that Africa was compelled to contribute to the development of this country. In this respect the United States gave less in return for what she took than any other power. By contrast, the European powers, at least, through their colonizing, implanted the seeds of change and modernization.

World War II awakened America to the importance of Africa as well as the rest of the colonial world. There followed a decade Coleman has called "reluctant involvement"[4] growing out of the necessities of the postwar settlement and the threats to the predominant United States role presented by the spread of revolutionary communism. This situation gave a primary security orientation to American policy concerns that expressed itself in attempts to secure the crumbling position of the colonial powers from Egypt to the Rhodesian Federation. Thus, significant United States involvement in Africa came as a result of the security system that was hastily constructed after the collapse of postwar hopes of cooperation with the Soviet Union in building a peaceful world. The new role for the United States cannot be encompassed by the ideological interpretation of the United States as an imperialist capitalist power in Africa. The small but growing American economic interest was limited to areas such as Libya, South Africa, Liberia, and Zambia. Later, Angola and Nigeria acquired some significance. The motives for American involvement lay in the changing status of the Suez Canal, the search for secure air bases and tracking stations, and a general concern for governmental stability in the face of revolutionary threats. Thus, from 1950-1960 the United States viewed Africa as a key continent to maintain in the status quo against the threat of communist revolution. The Kennedy era corresponded to the sudden appearance of numerous new African states and brought a new subtheme of positive involvement on behalf of African identity. But the continuance of a strong colonial presence in southern Africa created an acute dilemma in American policy on nonalignment. President Kennedy hoped United States programs could be freed from their European orientation. Toward this end, he staffed the Africa Bureau of the State Department well, and placed at its head Governor G. Mennen Williams, who had been a powerful political figure in his own right though minimally knowledgeable about Africa. Other agencies such as AID and the Peace Corps received budgetary and staff support from the White House. African heads of state such as Nkrumah, Balewa, Touré, Haile Selassie, and many others were given full honors in their White House visits.[5]

Nevertheless, security considerations remained uppermost. The United States was allied to Western Europe. African nonalignment appeared to weaken Western Europe that the United States sought to strengthen against the Soviet threat, and an independence policy for southern Africa seemed to threaten the security linkages of the West in the South Atlantic and Indian oceans. Thus, in the last analysis, nonalignment was unacceptable to either the Kennedy or the Johnson Administrations. United States policy tried to straddle economic and military links with South Africa and Portugal and, at the same time, support independent African states who pledged themselves to the liberation of southern Africa. But when it came to the vital choices, United States power was always placed behind United States allies rather than the nonaligned.

The Congo crisis of 1960-1962 is an exception which was later reversed. Only the interests of a small member of NATO, i.e. Belgium, were at stake. If France or England had been the colonial power involved, the policy might well have held to the norm of the Alliance policy.

Allegiance to this Alliance policy was not limited to the military branch of policy-making. A powerful group of hard-liners has held sway in the highest echelons of the State Department. George Ball, Under-Secretary of State in the Kennedy and Johnson Administrations, is representative of this group. Its thinking is motivated primarily by a concern for the primacy of Western Europe in a grand strategy. As Ambassador Ball made perfectly clear in his lucid exposition of this thesis in *The Discipline of Power*,[6] the structure of power which will serve American interests in respect to Africa is a "closed system" as he terms it, of Western European primacy in Africa.[7] This is the old sphere of influence thesis which makes Africa subordinate to our Western European allies in American policy. Thus, during the Kennedy years what had been a dilemma became a glaring contradiction of policies. The United States allocated power on the basis of the old thesis of Western European primacy but welcomed the independence of African states in principle. It could paste over some of its inconsistencies as long as the issue was the independence of black Africa. But when the major issue became the white dictatorships of southern Africa (who are closely associated with Western Europe), and the self-rule of the African majority, the dilemma became an hypocrisy.

Sources of the Alliance

One of the earliest indications of the nature of American practice following World War II arose over Moroccan independence. During a wartime visit to North Africa, President Roosevelt promised the Sultan of Morocco, Mohammed V, that if he supported the Allied cause he would have American support for independence in the postwar world.[8] The United States never fulfilled this promise as the debates over Moroccan independence at the United Nations clearly demonstrated.[a] This failure resulted from the postwar NATO alliance which France and the United States joined following the Allied victory. With the turn toward a confrontation with the Soviet Union by 1946 and the announcement of the Truman Doctrine for Greece, the die was cast in the Mediterranean. The United States built important air bases in Morocco and acquired the use of naval facilities at Port Lyantey. The American strategic view of the entire African continent was well described by Admiral Richard L. Connolly, who wrote an article in 1955 on "Africa's strategic significance" in which he concluded, "Let us hope that our statesmen and military leaders of the future can prevent the loss to Communism and domination by the Soviet Union of the second largest continent — Africa."[9] In this article, he pointed to the importance of naval and land bases and communications networks. North Africa was singled out as a prime source of manpower and a proven fall-back point and invasion launching pad into Europe.[10]

Other major security points Admiral Connolly stressed were the Suez Canal, the ports of Masawa, Djibouti, Mogadisco, Mombasa, and Diego Suarez (which was then Madagascar) and, of course, the naval ports of South Africa. With the closing of the Suez Canal and the growth of Russian presence in the Mediterranean after the Arab-Israeli War of 1967, some strategists have emphasized the importance of South African naval bases. General S.L.A. Marshall (the brother of Charles Burton Marshall), in a brief study prepared for the American-African Affairs Association, clearly considers South Africa a member of the Western Alliance because of her strategic importance and industrial capacity.[11] He maintained that the Simonstown base is the only adequate naval facility controlling the Indian Ocean left to the United States and the Western world. He pointed out, too, that NATO naval contingents including South Africa conduct annual naval exercises, and argued that the Simonstown base is indispensable to the protection of the sea lanes of the southern Atlantic and the Indian Ocean. The paper is a polemical attack on those who seek to isolate South Africa, and reports that he asked two former Chairmen of the Joint Chiefs of Staff and one former-Secretary of Defense whether, in view of South Africa's security significance, America's best interests were served by "making an enemy of that state?" Even if discounted for the weighted character of the question, their strong negative replies doubtlessly reflect the thinking of this strategically oriented group. Actual American policy has been based far more upon the propositions that General Marshall propounds than upon the liberal principles of "sanctions against South Africa" that he attacks.

Although Africa is the only continent where the United States did not build an official military alliance system to function as SEATO does in Asia, CENTO

[a]At no time did the United States support directly the attempts of the Afro-Asian states to raise the issue of the independence of Morocco and other North African States at the United Nations. Morocco became independent in 1955.

does in the Middle East, and NATO does in Europe, the United States had no less interest in its strategic dimension. Such a system was not necessary because the United States was allied directly with the European powers who controlled that continent during the fifties. These powers were not anxious to have the United States intercede between them and their colonies and the fledgling independent states of Africa. They demanded that all policy and security relationships with their dependent African territories be cleared through their own colonial offices. The United States complied with this policy until the emergence of the independent African states, although the interests of the former metropolitan powers continued to be recognized scrupulously.[12]

The legal provisions of the NATO agreement stipulated that American arms would not be used outside the European theatre. However, colonial armies fought colonial wars in Africa with American arms. French transfer of American equipment to Algeria during that seven-year war was the most flagrant example of this. Portugal probably could not have sustained her conflict with the growing insurgent movements beyond a year or two without the NATO weapons and the financial support from the United States that enabled her to divert other resources to the costly colonial conflicts in Africa.[13]

The United States has, of course, supported United Nations military sanctions against South Africa and economic sanctions for Rhodesia. However, this support should be seen in the perspective of the ability of these regimes to obtain what they need elsewhere through other members of the Western Alliance such as West Germany and France.[b] United States attempts to curb the activities of close associates in supplying Rhodesia and South Africa have been purely perfunctory.[14] France has continued to supply South Africa with arms and technical advice of military significance despite the United Nations ban.

Political strategists have dismissed the suggestion that a naval blockade be made of Portuguese ports supplying oil and other commodities to Rhodesia, on the grounds that it would not work.[15] Uppermost in the minds of objectors is the significant change in our relationship to South Africa that such a step would inevitably entail. Obviously, South Africa could not participate in the annual NATO maneuvers in the southern Atlantic. Moreover, this view is primarily concerned about the uncertain character and loyalties of the successor regime if the white dictatorship were to fall.

Thus, in numerous significant ways, the strategic considerations of American policy have claimed top priority and constantly conflicted with the stated goals of American leaders and the general principles of self-determination and equality.

A Questionable Doctrine

The primacy of security and alliance is a questionable doctrine on several counts. Africa has not been threatened with invasion by a Communist power. Even more significant, no Communist government has come to power in Africa. Nonalign-

---

[b]Some doubts exist about France in a showdown, but she is considered anti-Communist and therefore a reliable Western European power if no longer an avowed ally.

ment holds sway from the Nile to the Zambezi. Even the most radical of the nonaligned nations have not formed alliances with the Soviet Union. The radical nonaligned states of Africa have moved away from Western and United States dependency but have not become the dependencies of Communist powers.

Even if it were true that during the heydey of Soviet expansion an alliance policy strengthening the West was justifiable, that condition no longer exists. The fragmentation of the Eastern bloc, de-Stalinization, and the rise of the rival Chinese power have all contributed to the necessity of a new policy. With the recession of the danger of a major atomic clash between the United States and the Soviet Union has faded the significance of a threat from revolutionary and even communist governments in Africa. The idea that a communist coup in some remote African country would constitute a direct threat to the security of the United States is not credible today. This reality has become accepted among some high State Department officials, though only a few Congressmen would publicly recognize it. Moreover, the powers with whom the alliance policy was first contracted have lost much of their traction in Africa, and France cannot be considered a reliable NATO ally any longer.

The grand design is coming apart at many points, as in NATO and SEATO. However, those who have designed a policy when faced with the collapse frequently become more tenacious rather than reconsider their assumptions.

New Directions

In response to the changes that have occurred in Africa and in the international system, the United States is capable of developing a new relationship with Africa. Yet hopeful directions that this new relationship might take could be blocked if old concepts such as European primacy are not abandoned.

Africa is one of the few areas of the world where the United States is not caught in a network of traditional interests from which it is almost impossible to extricate itself. Thus, a new direction for the United States in Africa is possible, provided its policy-makers are not wedded to the status quo.

Support for Nonalignment

Positive support of Africa as a nonaligned continent is a priority area of redirection. This means that the steps new African states have taken toward the creation of nonaligned policies should be encouraged. The United States must work out proper policies to promote nonalignment. It must establish, far more clearly than in the past, the very broad boundaries within which it recognizes that nonalignment may operate. This would not mean the acceptance of all claims to nonalignment or all approaches to this status as equally valid. Nor would this mean that the United States set its own standards. But a genuine recognition of the systemic characteristic of the nonalignment system needs to take place, and the behavior of nations assessed against these standards.

These criteria should include the four basic characteristics of nonalignment: (1) economic diversification, (2) military independence from any single power, (3) cultural and ideological African identity as distinct from any major power, and (4) diplomatic mediation between the great powers in the interests of peace and justice.

An independent and nonaligned Africa would not weaken Europe but could strengthen it by removing counter-revolutionary warfare drains on European economies, and by forcing the United Kingdom into closer cooperation with Europe. The acceptance of a nonaligned African continent would not mean the withdrawal of United States influence in the area. As noted above, intervention operates at many levels and American attempts to influence developments through cultural, economic, and educational programs is welcomed widely, as long as it does not seek to be exclusive. Most nonaligned African states are anxious to have the great powers confirm their friendship through legitimate economic aid programs administered in the open.

Each of the four major characteristics of nonalignment needs to be understood more fully and related to American policy. Economic diversification of trade and aid programs as well as the integration of small economies into larger regional and pan-African patterns are the necessary principles for strong, independent, and nonaligned African state economies. These principles have not guided economic aid and trade policies in Africa. Without denying the significance of United States aid contributions in education and technical services, we must recognize, nevertheless, that the thrust has been, first, toward opening new sources of trade for United States firms, and second, toward consolidating Western economic interests on the grounds that the Western Alliance promoted stability and the best hope for growing prosperity. The flow of aid and trade patterns between the United States and Africa clearly shows that over the past ten years the vast proportion of aid has gone to countries which have a close identification of interest with the United States and the Western world. Liberia, Ethiopia, South Africa, Morocco, Tunisia, Libya, Ghana, Sudan, Congo, and Kenya have received the lion's portion of United States aid.[c] After independence in 1960 and until the outbreak of the civil war, Nigeria became the principal beneficiary of United States aid. Countries who became critics of the West, such as Egypt and Ghana, once recipients of much aid, had been almost eliminated until the military coup against Nkrumah in 1966 restored Ghana to grace. Since then Ghana has been high on the list of recipients once more.[d] The gradual reduction of United States aid programs since the high point of 1962 has affected the capacity of the United States to broaden its involvement in Africa. In 1967 the Johnson Administration announced a regionalization plan for economic aid, known as the Korry Plan. This plan has had the effect, although not consciously intended, of restricting further United States aid programs to the support of "friendly" economies. In North Africa, Morocco has been selected as the hub of a Maghreb regional scheme. In West

[c]South Africa was the highest recipient of export-import bank loans between 1946-1965 — $152,800,000; Liberia was second with $88,700,000.

[d]A $19,992,000 loan was made in 1967 and a $14,994,000 loan in 1968.

Africa, Senegal and the Ivory Coast are the centers, and in Central Africa, the Congo (Kinshasa) has special priority despite the threat it presents to a functioning integration scheme of Sudan-belt countries in the UDEAC.

The desirability of all regional integration schemes is open to question. The customs unions and financial schemes initiated under colonialism and perpetrated by dominant European interests do not necessarily benefit African development.

The terms of these original agreements, such as those in the West African Customs Union and the East African Common Services Organization, invariably favored certain countries, i.e., the Ivory Coast and Kenya with their entrenched European business groups. Questions and reservations can be raised concerning the present structure of nearly every regional scheme where regional forms reflect the dominant role of states like the Ivory Coast and Kenya. Different political principles such as nonalignment might well lead to a different kind of regional pattern with other states selected as key development agents. One such case is Tanzania, which might well be selected as the key integrator of a broad East and Central African regional scheme that would include Zambia, Burundi, and Rwanda, and conceivably the southern Sudan and eastern Congo. Another integrative unit might well develop a pattern around Guinea with Liberia, Sierra Leone and Portuguese Guinea (liberated sections). The logical transportation route to the coast for much of this region lies through Guinea and Liberia.[16]

However, such schemes are currently contrary to the direction of American supported regionalism which, for example, threatens Guinea with a complete withdrawal of support unless it associates itself with financial and trade regionalism centered in either Senegal or the Ivory Coast. Guinea cannot accept this because of the close identification of both of these countries with the CFA and the French Banking System as well as with the EEC.[17]

United States aid programs should not be tied to any existing pattern of regional development. Some integration programs promote growth; others retard it. Regionalism should be subsumed within a pattern of total development of individual national units within a growing network of continental intra-African trade and development. African development should move simultaneously in expanding external trade and internal trade. Like a tree, it should extend its roots into the soil as its branches reach outward. This botanical analogy is sound economically as well as politically. Perhaps the early proponents of Pan-African economic integration were naive in estimating the difficulties, but a network of functional cooperation has begun to grow under ECA and OAU auspices.

A common market arrangement over a much broader pattern than present regionalism envisions is feasible provided the market is planned rather than free. These are not utopian dreams but very practical economic goals proposed by many thoughtful African leaders as well as economists. They have learned to adapt their political goals to economic necessities. If economic diversification of aid and trade patterns will in the long run result in a more productive system as well as greater political independence, this is the direction African political leaders will take.

A final caveat on United States economic policy in Africa must raise issue with a general reduction in all types of economic assistance to Africa. Since 1962 United States aid in Africa has dropped from the peak of $494 million to $298 million. Of course, this reflects in part a world-wide reduction of United States aid programs to the projected $1.9 billion for 1969. This retreat deprives United States aid administrators of the rudimentary tools and technicians to assist in significant development. If the cutback continues, despite our growing GNP and national budget, we can have very little hope of influencing the course of events in Africa significantly, no matter what policy the United States ultimately adopts.

But with an adequately financed program of aid, the United States can help Africa to develop the economic integration most suitable to regional conditions. In the long run, real economic strength will promote greater trade with the United States and more governmental stability.

Trade policies to support African economic growth have received inadequate attention. United States support for an equitable international stabilization fund for African exports such as coffee and cocoa could do more in a short time for stability for the total development programs of many African countries than all the loans and grants of the past.

United States trade with Africa, in many areas, is tied to the inefficient industries, cheap labor, and raw materials policies of Western European powers. Visionary leaders of United States industry are not content with the alliance policy that subordinates their interests to outmoded relationships. Therefore, their interest in new approaches through a nonaligned Africa policy is growing.

The second area in which a major shift would result if the United States were to adopt a nonaligned African policy is military lines of support. As we have noted, the United States has direct military links with a few countries. Outside of southern Africa, these are Liberia, Ethiopia, Libya, Morocco, and the Congo (K). The full extent of these ties is not known. The United States government is anxious that these links not be misinterpreted, and most of the African governments are sensitive to any suggestion that they are subordinate militarily to the United States. Liberia is the most dependent. Virtually her entire training program is provided by the United States and a mutual assistance treaty exists. The United States Air Force has certain landing rights at Monrovian airfields, and supplies most of Liberia's military planes and weapons.

Ethiopia is a primary American air base on the other side of the continent where a contingent of some 1,300 Americans operates out of a "training center" at Kagnew station in Asmara.[18]

The amicable withdrawal of the three United States air bases in Morocco (concluded by 1963) marked a growing recognition of the contradiction between African independence and nonalignment and the continuation of major bases on the African continent. This policy has been diluted by the process of subterfuge. "Tracking stations", "training centers", "landing rights", are not bases but represent significant military influence invariably reflected in policy. Another aspect of American military policy is the attempt to preserve Western military concessions in Africa to use as bases of supply and support in case hostilities break out. This Western Alliance policy extends beyond the southern African states to include the French in French Somaliland or Senegal, and the British in Nigeria.

Competition to supply arms to the nonaligned countries has become a major activity in Africa. Since the African states do not manufacture their own armaments, they must get them elsewhere. Standards are very difficult to adopt in what has become one of the most profitable and yet disreputable of businesses. Nonalignment can mean access to alternative sources of supply. Thus, the purchase of arms from Eastern Europe or China does not, in itself, violate nonalignment. A shift to sole dependence upon the Communist world for arms supply and training inevitably is suspect and therefore unwise for a state that wishes to be considered nonaligned, i.e., the UAR. The same can be said of the reverse action which was undertaken by Ghana following the military coup. A country which is aligned militarily to a great power has great difficulty sustaining other meaningful aspects of nonalignment. Great power maintenance of training missions and supply of arms is not contradictory with nonalignment, provided such programs do not attempt to monopolize the sources of supply and use them for political purposes in an interventionary manner. The tolerance levels for this kind of policy are very low. United States retraining of the Congolese Army under Mobutu is an example of such interventionary policies that create more difficulties than they solve.[e]

Because of the inevitable difficulties of enforcing codes of noninterventionary conduct by outside powers, the best method of controlling military intervention would be through a nonintervention agreement policed by an international agency. Such an arrangement would be in the interest of a United States policy supporting nonalignment as much as the nonaligned states involved. The United Nations Disarmament Commission could play a major role in this limitation of the arms race in Africa through international agreement.

American policy has very little real difficulty with the third category — recognition of African ideological and cultural identity. Generally, the United States has supported the emergence of African negritude identity in culture and African socialism. It has accepted the fact that African political culture, while influenced greatly by the Western world, will not imitate European patterns. Cold War thinking has encouraged this idea, as such African personality development was viewed as a means of preventing Communist ideologies from taking root. Thus, some American policy-makers have been more interested in the anti-Communist potential of African socialism and the African democracy ideas of Leopold Senghor and Julius Nyerere than in the significant content of their political philosophies.

A switch to support for African nonalignment might lead to deeper intellectual support for these assertions of the artistic and psychological side of the African personality. Since Afro-Americans constitute the largest group of overseas Africans and many of them are seeking to reestablish contact with their African heritage, this could well form the nucleus of major international

[e]The strong left-wing reactions in Stanleyville were, in part, a fear of the left toward the United States which was aggravated by counter-support from Communist powers.

exchange and mutual intellectual and cultural development. At present, these interests are on a public relations level operated by USIA, AID, and the Department of State. But a major educational and cultural program involving every level of American society might well be inaugurated by government and private associations. United States policy can explore several new directions in the realm of the fourth category — diplomatic mediation — to ease international tensions and settle international conflict. The OAU has not lived up to the high expectations of the early 1960's but it has a life of its own that brings it into the center of disputes just when it has been entirely discounted as ineffectual. United States policy has given general support to the idea of the OAU. But in practice it usually has been discounted and, on the occasion of the Stanleyville Drop, was bypassed.

Support for rival organizations (such as OCAM) against the radicals should have no part in United States nonalignment policy. The temptation to do this is strong when such groups support United States policy. The United States has hardly disguised its sympathies for the OCAM view of African problems. Rivalry between African camps has been intense, especially at times of international crises, and fission tendencies might split the OAU, encouraging rather than limiting international intervention. The strengthening of Africa's own problem-solving mechanisms as well as pan-African economic integration will promote the development of the African subsystem. As has been observed, no regional government is needed. Eventually, the gradual, functional growth of the OAU can transform the anarchy of competing states into a rational, cooperative, tension-resolving system. African states have made their clearest contribution to the mediation process on the universal level of the international system. Their role in disarmament conferences, the Pakistan-Indian War, the Arab-Israeli conflicts, the Vietnam War, and the Cuban Crisis has not always received the attention it deserved. Frequently, United States policy-makers have resented the refusal of African states to side with them during major crises. They have given few bouquets to African statesmen following an international crisis. A rare exception was the somewhat begrudging recognition of the work done by Ghana's Ambassador Quaison Sackey, who, as President of the General Assembly in 1965, skillfully maneuvered a settlement of the United Nations financial crisis caused by the impasse over apportionment for the Congo and Middle East Emergency Forces.

Few countries, particularly in the heat of an international crisis, can view objectively the role of those who attempt to mediate rather than support one side or the other. They generally discount the contributions of voices on the sidelines and claim credit for a settlement in terms of the skill of their own statesmen or the sheer power of their own position.

The development of a strong nonalignment contingent within the United Nations as part of the new international system is the most direct interest the United States has in promoting a nonaligned Africa. The shortcomings of the post-war collective security system have been painfully demonstrated. This system has been replaced partially by an informal negotiating system in which nonaligned and uncommitted states often act as important mediators. This time-honored method of diplomatic settlement has been magnified a thousand-fold in importance by the world-wide destructive nature of a nuclear war. A nuclear stalemate based upon mutual terror is very fragile unless some machinery for mediation and peaceful settlement exists. The United Nations is the obvious mechanism; yet the international ethos that surrounds it is as important as the agencies themselves. The nonalignment system made up of such subsystems as Africa may be the best lubrication for any international mechanism.

The United States should take a very positive approach to nonalignment. It should make every attempt to strengthen it. This involves giving it full recognition and credit for past and possible future accomplishments. To formalize the structure extensively might limit its operation, but clearer definition of the rules of the game would be most useful, and attempts should be made to persuade other great powers to recognize these rules. Wider representation of African states on international agencies and their inclusion in international conferences and international control commissions would strengthen the system further. Finally, more attention should be paid to the issues that directly concern the nonaligned countries. Trade agreements, aid programs, and human rights issues such as those in South Africa are ways of giving strength and recognition to the important new role of the nonaligned.

A basic United States objective should be to persuade other powers to support the nonalignment system. This would include the British and French as well as the Russians. Until the Chinese are brought into the international system in some way, it obviously will be impossible to gain their cooperation on anything of this magnitude.

A cardinal part of the establishment of a nonaligned African continent must be the withdrawal of extraneous and disruptive foreign influences that create competitive aligned systems on the continent. The outstanding example of this is the colonial and white supremacy regimes of southern Africa. If Africa is to be nonaligned and is to develop an integrative system for the continent, it must consist of self-determining, cooperating states from the Arab states of North Africa to the white minority dictatorships of southern Africa. The OAU must be able to reach from one end of the continent to the other and encompass within its system all states regardless of their racial and ethnic diversity. To permit antithetical regimes to exist is a major disruption of the system and a temptation to outsiders to intervene in conflicts on behalf of one side or the other. If the policy of a nonaligned Africa is to work, the southern African subsystem that directly contradicts all the principles of nonalignment must be dismantled. Western powers will have to withdraw their support of the South African subsystem and encourage in every way possible the formation of African majority-based governments. This will not be done easily, and considerable force and persuasion will be necessary. But to say that it cannot be done is a curious kind of defeatism usually propounded by those who advocate much more unrealistic objectives such as protecting South Vietnam from Communism, for which they have recently committed the United States to the expenditure of more than $30 billions a year and tens of thousands of American lives.

Former American Ambassador to the United Nations Arthur Goldberg revealed after his resignation that he supports such a policy of disengagement from white supremacy. Apparently he could not gain acceptance for these views while he was in office. The former ambassador suggested a number of concrete steps on southern Africa to be taken: a stricter arms embargo on South Africa to close the export loopholes; use our influence on Japan and France to halt their sales; close our missile and space-tracking stations in South Africa; reexamine our nuclear cooperation agreement; cease naval refueling stops; end export-import loans and actively discourage private loans and business transactions; and end the South African sugar quota.[19]

He also urged "visible disengagement from Portugal in the Portuguese ruled African territories. . . . "[20] This disengagement thesis is not the total boycott program of the African states, although it is a step in that direction. It meets the Ball thesis on the grounds that it is not "a romantic illusion" aimed at bringing the South Africans, Rhodesians, and Portuguese to their knees. If vigorously applied, it will weaken the white dictatorships and speed the internal processes of revolution by the African majority.[21]

White supremacy in southern Africa can be defeated by a concerted policy that need not entail the direct use of military force. The system maintains itself primarily on the alliance it has built with the Western world. This alliance is crumbling, as demonstrated. Once Western support is withdrawn the entire psychological base of the system will be destroyed and its other exterior supports will begin to crumble rapidly. Southern Africa thrives on the present Western Alliance policy of the United States toward Africa. A shift to a nonalignment policy will set new forces in motion that may well force its disintegration more quickly than had been thought possible previously. Once Western support is withdrawn the white supremacy system would visibly begin to break down, and the African liberation forces gathering on the borders of the southern African system would be able to move forward to destroy it with minimum loss of life to all racial groups concerned.

The wealth and power of the United States should be used to prepare the liberation movements for their future responsibilities as governing authorities. This would include financial backing for education and training of various liberation cadres. Private agencies have been granting assistance for education and training.[f] The liberation groups can purchase arms themselves on the world market, and the United States need not become involved directly in this questionable traffic.

The types of activities that can be considered legitimate and effective is a complex matter entailing practical as well as moral considerations. The tendency of many guerrilla operations to operate on the principle "the end justifies the 'means" cannot be accepted. Force restrained by humanistic considerations must always apply whether that force is being used against black men or white men,

---

[f]There is no necessity for covert activity. The United States government can make grants directly to such groups as the International Defense and Aid Fund, as other governments have done.

Western or non-Western. In this respect the United States herself will need to be nonaligned and function as an impartial arbitrator.

Winds of Change

The prospects of a shift in United States policy from the alliance system to a nonalignment approach do not appear very bright at this writing. While the winds of change are continuing to blow through the revolutionary areas of the world, the United States has politically exhausted its resources and lost its idealism in the tragic blunder of Vietnam. This has drastically affected our capacity to respond with innovation and spirit to new ventures elsewhere. The Nixon Administration is reflective of this in its cautious approach to foreign affairs, speaking in moralistic tones but venturing nothing beyond the established boundaries.

This withdrawal and drift can change with time, but it will eventually take a major shift of political forces within the country to recognize the necessity of a new policy. Several major new social forces are stirring within the American political system that could in time help bring such a change.

One of the hopeful new forces is the rising power of Americans of African ancestry who when aroused about African issues, take quite a different view of American responsibilities than do the advocates of European primacy. This view is sensitive to the injustices and poverty of the African majority and instinctively hostile to the interests of a white supremacy system. Black American leaders in increasing numbers are equating their own search for dignity and full equality with the aspirations of the black Africans.[22] Differences of culture and nation have been barriers to this identification in the past, and will probably never entirely disappear, yet the growing militancy of American blacks has given a tremendous impetus to this trend.[23]

The influence that American blacks will have on American foreign policy will depend a great deal on the growth of their political powers. Evidence that the black is becoming a more potent political force is quite clear, from the party registration drives in the South to the capture of city machines in the North. The disruptive activities of the militants has also been a factor. There is, of course, the strong danger that the militants can precipitate a reaction that may for a time isolate and reduce black power. But unless the American political system is drastically altered, the impact of 20 million black Americans organized into political groups will be substantial.

The influence American ethnic groups have had on the course of American foreign policy has generally been emotional and disruptive of the general interest of the nation. Pressures of German, Irish, Polish, and Jewish Americans all at different times and circumstances reveal this fact.[24] They are prone to press their special interests and ties at the expense of reasonableness and restraint. The history of black American participation in foreign policy is likely to be similar unless more rapid adaptation to these interests is undertaken by enlightened groups in American society.

Other groups are beginning to stir. One of the most potent groups, when it becomes aroused, is made up of the churches. Their influence is more indirect than direct, but it stems from the creation of a climate of moral concern. This climate, in the past, has been generally supportive of the paternalistic and security-conscious character of American policy, because of the missionary domination of the churches' foreign activities. Mission boards have had the major contacts with Africa and have channeled American church resources into the field. Under the changes of independence, both of nations and churches in Africa, this relationship has been significantly altered. The predominant voices are no longer those who proclaim the Christianizing and civilizing mission of the West. A new interest in the moral well-being and material development of the peoples of Africa has emerged. Acts of great power intervention and the establishment of white racist regimes have come under increasing criticism. Such concern finds an outlet in increasing educational programs that relate Christian and religious principles to the fulfillment of self-determination aspirations. And a growing number of liberal church agencies have launched attacks against the use of American financial and political power to sustain white minority dictatorships, such as the recent campaign against American banks that underwrite loans to the South African government.[25]

Within American universities and foundations can also be found a growing group of dissidents who deplore the Alliance policy as a basis of the use of American power in Africa. Small in number but well informed and influential, this group should not be discounted.

Nevertheless, a major shift in American policy is not likely without a major change of internal political patterns. Pressures within the American society, particularly in the ghettos and among the disadvantaged nonwhite minorities are growing to the point where a major shift must take place or the American democratic political system may no longer be viable. When this comes, it may well be closely associated with major changes in American foreign relations. Then the prospect may become bright for a substantial shift away from the old military alliance concepts that underwrite present American policy toward Africa. The alternative suggested in this book can then become a serious contender: disengagement from white racism in southern Africa and support for the emerging nonaligned African subsystem.

10 Nonaligned Black Africa and World Peace

The aspiration for peace is a world-wide longing shared by all peoples and most political leaders. Because people also want other things, such as economic advancement and territorial recognition, differing ideas of social justice can lead to conflict between rival groups. Yet as these clashes have led to increasingly destructive warfare in our time, the yearning for peace grows.

The advent of many new states with new ideas and interests has led to a great deal of expectation concerning improved prospects for world peace. Much of this has been based upon idealistic hopes that are so detached from reality as to lead to inevitable disillusionment.

The Third World has not brought the peace its exponents had hoped it would; it has, in fact, brought many new conflicts. However, the emerging nations have changed the character of the international system and transformed the old institutions of world order into agencies of change never anticipated by those powers who created them after World War II. The primary question is, whether this increased participation in the world system and the new institutions can cope with the new problems any more successfully than earlier periods.

Peace, for the peoples of Africa, as well as for the peoples of the great powers and the rest of the world, is now obviously interrelated. In developing the concept of nonalignment, African leaders have been acutely aware that the position of small powers has an impact upon the international system just as they are in turn affected by the character of the international system itself. One kind of international system might mean war in Africa, or in the world, whereas another kind of international system could create the environment in which their hopes for rapid development could be fulfilled.

Likewise the leaders of the great powers have, as we have seen, been forced to adapt their policies to the realities of the change in social situation in Africa. Although they may view Africa as a secondary area of interest, the interrelatedness of this continent with the total global pattern of peace is undeniable. Therefore the pursuit of peace must be seen within the pattern of interaction between the nonaligned African subsystem and the international system itself. This is a very elaborate pattern of interrelationships and interaction can be considered here only in a general way.

Instability, conflict, and war are apt to characterize international relations for some time to come. What is important, though, is the prospect for minimizing this destruction and promoting a more tolerable condition for human life and growth.

Great Powers in Africa

To what extent have the new African states over the past decade played a role in the important decisions related to war and peace? The answer to such a question depends a great deal upon the conception of the viewer of the character of the international system and the weight given to several variables, as contributing to war and peace.

Some analysts give heavy emphasis to the international order variable and others consider the balance of military power to be the key to maintaining peace.

This work has employed the systems approach that contrasts in basic assumptions with the realist school in several points. The most important has been the view of the world as a plural power system in which the Cold War, for many nations, is not the basic organizing motif. While the Cold War constitutes an important issue area for a large number of nations, there are numerous other issues such as poverty, color, religion, and cultural identity that have determined more basically the international behavior of many other nations. Thus when issues such as South Africa or raw material commodity agreements are raised, these issue areas of race and poverty come into operation and determine the behavior of the new African states, far more than the rivalry between the United States and the Soviet Union over respective control in Berlin.

From this perspective, it is seen that the approach of most African states to the major conflicts of the world outside of the African area is quite different from the great powers and they frequently have a different perspective on the conflicts between small powers, as in the Middle East and Asia.

Despite this difference of interest and interpretation, they play a role by virtue of their number, unity, and place within international agencies, especially the United Nations. There are a vast variety of ways in which the African states have sought to exercise this influence, and with exceedingly varied results, ranging from a resolution of the OAU or the African caucus at the United Nations, to private diplomatic pressure between heads of state during formal receptions.

A certain range of problems has been particularly susceptible to the multilateral African diplomacy. When the issue has been an African one, the collective voice of African states has been most effective, as in pressuring the British in the Rhodesian UDI crisis or the United States over the Congo. We have seen, however, the limits within which this pressure has been effective. When the issue is non-African, the African states have clearly been more divided and less influential.

Issues of less immediate importance to the great powers themselves have been most conducive to African and small power intercession. Such matters as the recognition of Communist China by Great Britain and France clearly have been influenced by the attitude of African states, though this should be seen as only one factor in the decision to recognize China. Joseph Murumbi, the Foreign Minister of Kenya, expressed the view of the African states which supported the admission of China to the United Nations, "It is evident more than ever today that without the Peoples' Republic of China, no peace in South East Asia can be secured. Without it the usefulness of the United Nations will always be limited."[1] However, when the question of what to do with Nationalist China arises, African solidarity on this issue breaks. The radicals support expulsion, while the moderates vote for a two-China solution.

The ban on atmospheric testing of nuclear devices has also been influenced to some extent by the strong protests of African states who condemned testing on African soil and the universal polluting of the atmosphere. The nonproliferation treaty also received strong support from many countries, such as Ethiopia, Ghana, Ivory Coast, Liberia, Nigeria and Tanzania, who introduced a resolution in the United Nations First Committee in 1965, calling for "a treaty to prevent the proliferation of nuclear weapons." Tanzania and Zambia later opposed the nonproliferation treaty on the grounds that it made the nuclear powers "an exclusive club" and sincere steps toward disarmament were not being taken.[2] However twenty-four African states supported the Treaty.

During the direct confrontation of great powers that threatened to break out into hot war (like the 1961 Berlin crisis and the Cuban crisis of 1962), the role of the small African powers has been restricted to the sidelines. They can do little more than urge restraint and negotiation, though this in itself is important at times.[3]

When a great power is not itself directly involved in a crisis, as the United States in the Suez Crisis of 1956, the opinions of the African and Third World powers may exert a very strong influence. President Eisenhower's desire not to allow the Russians to become the dominant power in the Arab world of the Middle East and North Africa clearly influenced the United States decision to oppose the British, Israeli, and French invasion of the Suez.[4] In a similar manner the views of the French and the British on United States involvement in Vietnam after the Geneva Conference of 1954 were prone to influence from the new African states as well as all the other non-Western powers who opposed this intervention because they viewed it not as a struggle against communism but a United States attempt to maintain a dominant position in Vietnam and the Pacific.

The most important role of small powers in international crises has arisen when the great powers have decided not to seek a military settlement and to negotiate the dispute. At this point they are willing and frequently anxious to allow the international machinery of the United Nations to come into operation and welcome the conciliatory role of the small, nonaligned powers. Settlements of number of crises have been greatly facilitated by the participation of the small powers, including African states. Both Ghana and the UAR during the Cuban crisis, as members of the Security Council, participated in a number of discussions that devised a formula for the Soviet Union to extricate itself from this impasse.[5] The point of view reflecting a desire for compromise was started by Mr. Karefa-Smart, Representative of Sierra Leone: "My delegation notes with great apprehension the storm clouds which are developing on this side of the Atlantic over Cuba. Since we believe that there is universal agreement among us that each member state has the sovereign right to choose its own form of government, we urge both the United States Government and the Soviet Union to refrain from interfering in Cuba's internal affairs and from armed intervention over Cuba. Any act on either side leading to warfare today is folly. . . ."

While the capacity of Africans to prevent the conflict was very limited, their refusal to back either side helped the United Nations to create a framework in which the Soviet Union could honorably withdraw from a dangerous position.[6]

African countries were not active in the 1954 Geneva accords that led to French withdrawal from Vietnam, as only two were independent at that time. During the various phases of American intervention in the Vietnam war, African states have attempted to provide mediation facilities. Nkrumah, as a spokesman for the Commonwealth, was especially active in seeking to provide good offices. Among the pragmatically nonaligned African states, Ethiopia has been the most outspoken on behalf of a settlement. The Ethiopian delegate, Katema Yifra, expressed a widely held African attitude: "We believe that the people of Vietnam, both North and South, should be left alone to determine whatever social structure, form of government, or philosophy of state they deem fit for their nation."[7]

Since several of the radical nonaligned African states have diplomatic ties with Hanoi and Peking as well as contact with the NLF, they have been useful as intermediaries. The necessity for independent international supervision of whatever accords are finally agreed upon between the disputing parties may well involve several of the more diplomatically influential African states such as Ethiopia, Tanzania and Tunisia.

The impact of African states on the United Nations has been a major one in terms of their influence on the growth and funding of United Nations technical and economic agencies. The specialized agencies increased their budgets by 173 percent from 1960 to 1967. And such new agencies as the United Nations Conference on Trade and Development were created during this period when African states were exerting growing influence.[8]

On such matters as international commodity price control and measures to correct the trend toward unfavorable terms of trade for African countries, Africans have been especially active. Regional arrangements, such as associate states with the EEC have been achieved, and certain powers have made favorable trade arrangements as a part of an economic aid program.

However, African and other underdeveloped nations were unsuccessful in persuading the great powers to undertake any major reforms in international trade or to fund these new agencies. The failure of the New Delhi UNCTAD Conference demonstrated very clearly this impasse between the underprivileged and the affluent nations. Thus, while the forty-two independent African states (as of mid-1969) have added substantially to the numerical majority the new nations now enjoy in such conferences, their economic power has been insufficient to extract major concessions. This has created a great source of aggravation, especially as most African states have shifted their priorities in foreign policy from Cold War political crises to the bread and butter issues. Most African states are convinced that in the long run world peace will be jeopardized more by the failure of the great powers to meet the economic expectations of emergent peoples than by the arms race or the expansion of aggressive communism. In the words of the Guinean Minister of Foreign Affairs, "The numerous attempts made by the imperialist powers to establish economic communities and military alliances do not lead to a true and equal solidarity among free and equal partners, but only keep the poor in poverty and the slave enslaved."[9]

The most promising areas of activity for African states and other small powers in influencing long-term peace factors have been in the area of international technical agreements and covenants covering the activities of all powers. African states have been in the forefront of those requesting international agreement on the use of space and the development of the seabed. In the latter case, fishing and mineral rights are directly affected for the small powers of Africa. It is very much in their interests to gain agreement on the extent of the continental shelf and the uses of the ocean before conflicts with and between great powers arise. As independent entities, they are in a much stronger position to obtain better terms than they were under colonial rule.

There has been a great deal of discussion concerning a nonintervention covenant that would specify the types of intervention and clearly limit the ways they might be employed. Great powers are prepared at least to consider a convenant that would only commit them to support a principle. The interest of the African powers lies in making any such agreement that emerges as specific as possible, with automatic inspection and enforcement procedures. At least great powers have begun to listen. To some extent they are deterred from precipitous interventionary action by a broadly based consensus among African states and other small powers concerning aggressive action. The difficulties of legal agreement on these matters should not be minimized. Nevertheless, certain general principles have begun to emerge on which there is a consensus, such as the priority of regional and multilateral procedures rather than unilateral force intervention.

The high priority African states have given to racial and colonial matters has been evidenced in their voting activity at the United Nations. Their preoccupation with these issues has frequently been interjected into separate issues such as South African membership on specialized agencies. Africans view such issues as South Africa and the Congo crisis as directly linked to keeping peace in the world. As has been stated many times above, a sharp difference of opinion on this matter exists between Africans and Western nations.

African states demand that resolutions be implemented through international action such as the withdrawal of the South West African Mandate from South

Africa, and the creation of a United Nations committee to take over the administration of the territory.

One observer has pointed out how African states at the United Nations have increasingly turned their attention to matters of direct concern to Africa. This has coincided with a tendency among many African states to abstain from the Cold War issues of world politics.[10] The demise of several radical leaders such as Nkrumah, Ben Bella, and Mdibo Kieta, who conceived of their function as "peacemakers" as well as nation-builders, has contributed to this trend.

The Third World Issue Area

Unity among the nonaligned touches upon a critical aspect of African influence on the behavior of great powers. Nkrumah was theoretically correct that great powers would give a united Africa greater attention than a divided one. From the start of independence the difficulty lay in achieving meaningful unity and in widening it out to include other nonaligned nations.

A great deal of mythology has been built around the Third World as an international system. Those seeking to emphasize its importance have exaggerated its character and influence. The Third World exists as a system only in an issue-area context. It has none of the features of an integrative problem-solving system of the nonaligned African subsystem. The various Afro-Asian conferences that have been held reflect the issue-area character of this system and not these other features. The membership of the Third World group has been very fluid so that no identity has been established. Even the polar states, such as India and Ghana, can no longer be identified as spokesmen for this group. The Third World does not caucus as a group at the United Nations. The major unifying theme is a point of view on colonial and racial issues.

However, this common perspective is not without major significance. It does mean that the African states can count on a substantial group of Asian support when it comes to a showdown over an explicit issue such as Rhodesian white supremacy. The Suez crisis of 1956 demonstrated to the great powers the unifying significance for Third World nations for anticolonial issues. This in itself has created an atmosphere of constraint upon unilateral uses of power. The Russians, in dealing with China, have had to take this into account, as they cannot afford to allow the Chinese to use anticolonialism and nonwhite solidarity feelings over the Manchurian and Mongolia territorial disputes. Moreover, even in a nuclear confrontation such as the Cuban crisis of 1963, Robert Kennedy reported that President Kennedy was clearly constrained in accepting the advice of the hardliners to bomb Cuba by his concern for the effects of such action on the uncommitted nations.[11]

African leadership and utilization of the Third World has not been effective. The attempts of more radical Africans to weld the Afro-Asian nations into a unified caucus group outside of particular issues has not been successful. Nongovernmental meetings of the Afro-Asian Peoples Solidarity Conference have been hardly more successful. Russian and Chinese rivalries conducted through their respective fronts and friendly parties have done more than anything to blunt the effectiveness of such activities. Liberation movements identified with the Chinese were excluded from the 1968 Khartoum Conference, dominated by the pro-Russian faction.[12]

The Third World is thus a buffer zone of issue-oriented former colonial states that respond within the global system in terms of a world view they have in common. The trend among these nations, as with the African states, is toward the narrowing of these concerns around regional economic development and the building of regional independence from great power dominance. Although more a shift of emphasis than a major change in nonalignment perspective, India's preoccupation with matters of direct concern to her own welfare rather than Third World programs for world peace is indicative of the new stance.

The 1970's

The global system of the 1970's is one that will be characterized by greater pluralism as contrasted with polarization. Under the impetus of the two major forces of the breakup of the great power blocs and the growth of nonaligned subsystems, the world is moving toward a greater diversity of power and ideology. Within such an international system, Africa will have more influence on events in Africa and play a major role within the world as a whole.

African nonalignment is a prime example of the trend toward pluralism in the world. As the African subsystem strengthens, it will become more capable of resolving African problems and less reliant upon outside intervention. The growth of regionalism in Europe, the Middle East, South Asia and Latin America are parallel developments in the changing international system.

Western powers are simultaneously disengaging their presence in such areas as Africa and withdrawing into narrower circles of interest. While the communist powers are still expanding into new areas of the world, they are greatly limited by the competition between the Soviet Union and the Chinese Peoples' Republic.

The world of the 1970's is apt to be one in which nonalignment and subsystems of small powers will thrive more easily than the Cold War pattern would permit during the 1950's and 1960's.

Tendencies toward fragmentation within nations and subsystems will continue, but as outside intervention is reduced, at least one major source of intraregional hostility will be lessened. This should not mislead African leaders into assuming that the path to the unity of Africa has thereby been cleared. Internal tensions are as much if not more important than external aggravations. The chances are that the tensions and conflicts based on ethnic and racial hostilities are going to increase with the rapid changes of the future. But they can be reduced in their impact and resolved more easily if they are localized rather than globalized.

A plural global system may well be a safer world for the more stable societies, as the dangers of a major conflict between the great nuclear powers will be correspondingly reduced. But for the less stable nations it might mean an increase in tensions and conflict at a lower level. With the withdrawal of the integrating force of great powers the prospects for secessionist groups are improved, and the temptations for many other dissident factions to rebel are greater because the retaliation would be less severe. Intervention by great powers who defend what they perceive as their own interests within internal wars is apt to increase in this kind of world.

The prospect that a nonaligned African subsystem can influence significantly the policies of great powers in the world is dependent upon the amount of unity and strength this subsystem develops. This influence cannot be that of great economic importance or military force. Great powers want to maintain good diplomatic ties and friendly relations in order to sustain their interests in the area and to prevent a sudden turn toward alignment with rival powers. The influence of a nonaligned African subsystem or that of individual nonaligned African states will thus be significant in the world system, but the direct impact cannot be measured accurately. There are two major variables in the nature of future conflicts between great powers, and the skill with which African leaders use their influence in the world arena.

The greatest contribution to world peace that the African states can make is to participate with other small powers in the gradual development of an international order of moral responsibility and the legitimization of defined procedure around the United Nations. Obviously, small powers can only push such development to a point where great power concurrence is needed in order to give reality to any international organization. After every crisis, where the great powers have ignored the accepted rules, small states can create an international atmosphere and an increasingly recognized multilateral method of settling disputes by persistent persuasion and patient reconstruction.

Small powers have already enabled the world to see that the cause of world peace can best be served not as much by institutions as by a general recognition that the final significant relationship is the human one. We are forced to function through national and regional systems, but in the end all men are a part of the global system. It is essential that we have respect for each other as human beings who have distinctive qualities of Africans, Europeans, or Asians. Mutual respect and recognition is the minimum we can ask of each other. We can hope for more but are not likely to find it in group relations in this world. The pursuit of separate interests is to be expected and conflict will result. However, if we are to continue to inhabit this planet we will have to agree upon limits to conflict. We will also need to demonstrate toward each other a far greater tolerance of diversity, and a keener senstivity to the global scope of injustices and inequities that have led to hostilities in the past. Strengthened political systems capable of resolving these kinds of problems at all levels are our best hope for peace.

Notes

Notes

Chapter 1
The Nonalignment Subsystem

1. See, for example, Michael Brecher, "International Relations and Asian Studies: The Subordinate State System," *World Politics,* January 1963; and I. William Zartmen, "Africa as a Subordinate State System in International Relations," *International Organization*, Summer 1967.

2. Quoted by Peter Worsley in *The Third World* (London: Widenfeld and Nicolson, 1964), p. 247.

3. *The New York Times*, Sept. 25, 1960, p. 36. This was not a casual remark; when asked about it later he stuck to his view.

4. J.W. Burton, *International Relations: A General Theory* (Cambridge: Cambridge University Press, 1965), pp. 149-150.

5. Kwame Nkrumah, *Neo-Colonialism: The Last Stage of Imperialism*, (London: Nelson, 1965), p. 254.

6. *West Africa*, 6 November 1965, p. 1247.

7. This, he believes, can only be due to a common world view he calls "neutralism." *Ibid.,* p. 232.

8. See Hans J. Morgenthau, *Politics Among Nations* (New York: Knopf, 1948); or A.F.K. Organsky, *World Politics* (New York: Knopf, 1958).

9. Herbert Spiro, *World Politics: The Global System* (Homewood, Ill.: The Dorsey Press, 1966), pp. 50-51. He presents four basic phases of the political process: 1) formulation, 2) deliberation, 3) resolution of issues, and 4) solution of problems, p. 51. I use an adapted form of these to define an international subsystem.

10. James Rosenau, "Foreign Policy as an Issue Area," in *Domestic Sources of Foreign Policy* (New York: The Free Press, 1967), pp. 12-13.

11. Among those theorists who are skeptical regarding the depth and content of neutralism is Peter Lyons, who nevertheless argues its importance must be accepted, as he says, "to admit that the doctrine is superficial in its arguments is not to deny its importance, appeal, or influence. . . . The ideas and feelings men have about events in which their lives are engaged are a dimension of the events themselves. . . ." Peter Lyons, *Neutralism* (Leicester: Leicester University Press, 1963). The persistence of this view among recent writers is demonstrated in Robert Rothstein's article, "Alignment, Non-Alignment and Small Powers," *International Organization*, Summer 1966. He argues nonalignment "is a tactical principle and that many have a 'disguised alignment' that will appear when they are attacked."

12. Cecil Crabb, *The Elephants and the Grass* (New York: Praeger, 1964); and J.W. Burton, *Nations in a Multi-Polar World* (New York: Harper and Row, 1968); and *Systems, States, Diplomacy and Rules* (Cambridge: Cambridge University Press, 1968).

13. Robert Rothstein makes this distinction clearly in "Alignment, Non-alignment, and Small Powers," *op. cit.*, p. 402.

14. *The African Phenomenon* (Boston: Allyn and Bacon, Inc., 1968), p. 133.

15. Burton argues that any state can be nonaligned. However, this writer believes that great powers may profess a nonalignment ideology but in practice

seek to subordinate lesser powers, thereby creating subordinate rather than nonaligned subsystems.

16. J.W. Burton, in his book, *International Relations: A General Theory* (Cambridge: Cambridge University Press, 1965), p. 2, says: "The world society is one in which there is an increasing independence of each of its units, each co-operating in regional and functional arrangements . . . . Non-alignment, looked at in this perspective is a relevant response to the conditions of the nuclear age."

17. See Michael Haas, "International Sub-systems: Stability and Polarity," unpublished paper delivered to the American Political Science Association, September 1968.

18. William Zartman uses these terms, *op. cit.*, p. 549.

19. Karl Kaiser notes this tendency when he states the proposition: "Overlapping regional sub-systems in which a super-power participates interact in such a way as to foster the formation of advanced forms of comprehensive regional sub-systems, excluding the super-power." "The Interaction of Regional Sub-systems," *World Politics*, Summer 1968, p. 105.

Chapter 2
The Racial and Colonial Origins
of African Nonalignment

1. See Paul F. Power (ed.), "Final Communique of Asian-African Conference in Neutralism and Disengagement" (New York: Scribner Research Anthologies, 1964), pp. 9-14.

2. See the earliest comprehensive study of these patterns in Thomas Hovet, *Africa at the United Nations* (Evanston, Ill.: Northwestern University Press, 1963).

3. Margaret Legum, "Africa and Non-alignment," in J.W. Burton, *Non-Alignment* (London: Andre Deutsch, 1966), p. 57.

4. Quoted in Peter Worsley, *The Third World* (London: Weidenfeld and Nicolson, 1964), p. 255.

5. Ali Mazrui, "African Political Attitudes and the United Nations," *East African Journal*, October 1964, p. 35.

6. Ali Mazrui, *Towards a Pax Africana* (Chicago: University of Chicago Press, 1967), p. 167.

7. In J.W. Burton, *Non-Alignment, op. cit.*, p. 57.

8. *The Race War* (New York: Viking Press, 1967).

9. Leopold Senghor, *On African Socialism*, (New York: Praeger, 1964), p. 165.

10. One of the more interesting recent studies of these African patterns at the United Nations is Benjamin D. Meyer's study, "African Voting in the General Assembly," *The Journal of Modern African Studies*, vol. 4, no. 2, pp. 213-229.

11. See James Coleman and Carl Rosberg, *Political Parties and National Integration in Tropical Africa* (Berkeley: University of California Press, 1964), p. 5.

12. *Ibid.*

13. Cited in G.W. Shepherd, *The Politics of African Nationalism* (New York: Praeger, 1962), p. 100.

14. See Tom Mboya, "African Socialism," *Transition,* vol. 3, no. 8; and Julius Nyerere, "Ujamaa," *Tanganyika Standard*, Dar es Salaam, 1960.

15. J.D.B. Miller, *The Politics of the Third World* (New York: Oxford, 1967),. p. 106.

Chapter 3
Regional Rivalries and Caucuses
within the African Subsystem

1. See Colin Legum, *Pan-Africanism*, rev. ed. (New York: Praeger, 1965), pp. 25-26.

2. I. Wallerstein's view of regional systems comes close to this when he says, "There have only been three serious movements toward regional unity and each is now defunct as a movement." However, he argues that the Pan-African movement remains a reality. *Africa the Politics of Unity* (New York: Random House, 1967), p. 114.

3. See Melville Herskovits, *The Human Factor in Africa* (Evanston, Ill.: Northwestern University Press, 1962).

4. For a general survey of the results see "New Trends in African Integration," *Africa Today,* vol. 15, no. 5(Oct./Nov. 1968).

5. See Albert Tevoedjre, *Pan-Africanism in Action* (Cambridge, Mass: Center for International Affairs, Harvard University, November 1965).

6. They are most completely represented in *Africa Must Unite* (New York: Praeger, 1963), pp. 132-172.

7. These have been documented by the Ankrah Government. Henry Bretton in his *Rise and Fall of Kwame Nkrumah* (New York: Praeger, 1967), p. 162, describes aptly the chief instrument of this revolutionary zeal, the Kwame Nkrumah Ideological Institute at Winneba by saying, "This he had intended as the central academy for training revolutionary ideologists to further the Nkrumist program for Ghana and for all Africa."

8. See Hella Pick, "The Brazzaville Twelve and How They Came to Be," *Africa Report*, May 1961.

9. For a full discussion of the activities of this group see Tevoedjre, *op. cit.*

10. I. Wm. Zartman, *International Relations in the New Africa* (Englewood Cliffs, N.J.: Prentice-Hall, 1966) p. 34.

11. See Joseph Sterne, "The Lagos Conference," *Africa Report*, February 1962, pp. 3-6.

12. See John Markakis, "The Organization of African Unity: A Progress Report," *Journal of Modern African Studies*, IV, 2, (1966), pp. 135-153.

13. William Zartman maintains this view in his *International Relations in the New Africa, op. cit.*, pp. 130-133. This view is contradicted at certain points by

the former Secretary-General of the UAM, Albert Tevoedjre, in his *Pan-Africanism in Action: An Account of the UAM* (Cambridge, Mass.: Center for International Affairs, Harvard University, Occasional Paper No. 11, 1965).

14. *West Africa* (30 October 1965), p. 1211.

15. Speeches of Alhaju Sir Abubakar Tafawa Balewa, *Nigeria Speaks* (Longmans of Nigeria, 1964), p. 113.

Chapter 4
White Intervention and Black African Reaction:
The Case of the Stanleyville Drop

1. See Richard Cottam, *Competitive Interference and 20th Century Diplomacy* (Pittsburg: University of Pittsburg Press, 1967), p. 44-45.

2. See Colin Legum, *The Congo Disaster* (London: Penguin, 1961); Jean Van Lierde, *La Pensée Politique de Patrice Lumumba* (Paris: Présence Africaine, 1963); Alan Merriam, *Congo: Background of Conflict* (Evanston, Ill.: Northwestern University Press, 1961); Conor Cruise O'Brien, *To Katanga and Back: A United Nations Case History*, (New York: Simon and Schuster, 1962); Ernest Lefever, *Uncertain Mandate; Politics of the United Nations Congo Operation* (Baltimore: Johns Hopkins Press, 1967), and his contribution to William G. Andrews (ed.), *The Politics of International Crises* (Princeton: Van Nostrand, 1969).

3. *West Africa*, no. 2276 (January 14, 1961), p. 31.

4. These clashes are described by the Chief of Staff, General H.T. Alexander in his book, *African Tightrope* (London: Pall Mall Press, 1965), pp. 33-91.

5. M. Crawford Young, "The Congo Rebellion," *Africa Report* (April 1965), p. 7.

6. Edouard Bustin, "The Quest for Political Stability in the Congo," in *Africa: The Primacy of Politics*, ed. Herbert Spiro (New York: Random House, 1966), p. 27.

7. William Attwood's account in *The Reds and the Blacks* (New York: Harper and Row, 1967) of his own role as U.S. Ambassador in negotiating with Kenyatta is highly informative.

8. Security Council, S/PV1170 (9 December 1964), p. 16.

Chapter 5
The Coming of Confrontation Over Race:
The Rhodesian Case

1. Rosenau pointed out "systematic analysis of the functioning of all types of political systems from local to national to international . . . are also converging on the finding that different types of issues elicit different sets of motives on the part of different actors in a political system, that different systems' members are thus activated by different issues, and that the different

inter-action patterns that result from these variations produce different degrees of systemic stability for each type of issue." "Foreign Policy as an Issue-Area." in *Domestic Sources of Foreign Policy*, ed. James Rosenau (New York, The Free Press, 1967), p. 14.

2. Larry Bowman, in "The Subordinate State System of Southern Africa," *International Studies Quarterly* (September 1968), outlines the major characteristics of this second system.

3. See Colin Leys, *European Politics in Southern Rhodesia* (Oxford: Clarendon Press, 1959), pp. 73-77.

4. See Johan Galtung for an elaboration of the social significance of this, in his article, "On the Effects of International Economic Sanctions: With Examples from the Case of Rhodesia," *World Politics* (Spring 1967).

5. B.V. Mtshali, *Rhodesia: Background to Conflict* (New York: Hawthorn Books, 1967).

6. *Ibid.*, pp. 63-64.

7. *New York Times*, December 23, 1966.

8. See *Africa Today*, Vol. 14, No. 2, p. 14.

9. *The Central African Examiner*, November 1964, p. 2, said in relation to Smith's "not in his lifetime" statement, "his intransigence reflects the intransigence of white Rhodesians as a whole. They recognize that compromise with the Africans will eventually lead to an African Government and this they are determined to resist to the bitter end."

10. Margery Perham, *The Rhodesian Crisis*, pp. 7-8.

11. Margaret Roberts, "Rhodesia: What are the Issues?", *Venture* (March 1967), p. 11.

12. White Paper Cmnd 3159, p. 2.

13. See Lawrence Fellows, "The British Blockade," *The New York Times*, April 19, 1966.

14. See UN S/PV 1338, and S/RES 232.

15. See *The New York Times*, December 17, 1966, p. 8.

16. *Ibid.*

17. *Africa Confidential* 16 (August 4, 1967), p. 2.

18. *Ibid.* 23 (November 17, 1967), p. 1.

19. *London Sunday Times*, September 3, 1967: "Union Carbide maintains a 130,000-ton stockpile in Lorenço Marques which is constantly replenished, but belongs to Rhodesian, South African or Portuguese companies."

20. R.T. McKinnel, "Sanctions and the Rhodesian Economy," unpublished paper delivered to African Studies Association, October 1968. *The Rhodesia Herald*, Nov. 27, 1968, reported that E.S. Newson, Chairman of Rhodesian Iron and Steel Corporation, warned of a "marked deterioration of the economic situation. . . . To be quite blunt, we can in the long term never hope to win this war."

21. *New York Times*, October 16, 1968, p. 13.

22. *The Times of Zambia*, August 3, 1967.

23. Organization of African Unity, ECM/Res, 10 September, 1964.

24. Organization of African Unity, AHG/Res 25/Rev 1, 22 October 1965.

25. Julius Nyerere, "Costs of Non-alignment," *Africa Report* (October 1966), pp. 62-4.

26. John Markakis, in his article "The OAU: A Progress Report," *op. cit.*, p. 147, takes note of these preliminary discussions and concludes that the Secretariat deliberated the matter and submitted the proposal.

27. Mtshali, *op. cit.*, p. 135.

28. Mezerik, *1966 Chronology*, pp. 52-53.

29. *International Seminar on Apartheid, Racial Discrimination and Colonialism in Southern Africa* (New York: United Nations Office of Public Information, August 1967), pp. 4-19.

30. *The UN Monthly Chronicle*, November 1967, p. 12.

31. *Ibid.*

32. S/RES/253/1968. *UN Monthly Chronicle*, June 1968, pp. 36-68.

33. *Africa Confidential*, 1966 Supplement to No. 24 (December 9, 1966).

34. *New York Times*, October 20, 1967, p. 16.

35. *UN Monthly Chronicle* Vol. 4, No. 8, August-Sept. 1967, p. 42.

Chapter 6
Southern African Liberation Movements:
The Turn to Violence

1. *African Apartheid News*, December 1967, p. 2.

2. Frantz Fanon, *Toward the African Revolution* (New York: The Monthly Review Press, 1967), p. 181.

3. "Conversation with Eduardo Mondlane," *Africa Report* (November 1967), p. 51.

4. See Gérard Chaliand, *Lutte armée en Afrique* (Paris, 1967).

5. There is an important difference in tactics here between the Cuban-style insurgency advocated by Debray in *Revolution in the Revolution*, and the careful preparation suggested by Chaliand.

6. See John Marcum, "Three Revolutions," *Africa Report* (November 1967), p. 21.

7. See William F. Buckley, Jr., "Must We Hate Angola?", *The National Review* (December 18, 1962), p. 468.

8. George Houser, "African Liberation Movements," *Africa Today* (August 1967), pp. 12-13.

9. See Marcum, *op. cit.*, for details on the highly complex struggle of rival leaders and organizations.

10. *Ibid.*, pp. 12-13.

11. Basil Davidson, "Mozambique: the Next UDI?", *Venture* 19, June 1967, p. 21.

12. *Ibid.* Davidson notes the affinity of some Portuguese settlers for South Africa.

13. Nathan Shamuyarira, "The Majority Parties: 2) ZANU," *Venture* (October 9, 1965), p. 29.

14. The growing number of guerrilla operations is described by Patrick Keatley in the *Manchester Guardian Weekly*, July 25, and August 1st, 1968.

15. *Anti-Apartheid News*, November 1967, p. 3.

16. Colin Legum, *Pan-Africanism, op. cit.*, p. 8. The appearance of the African Resistance Movement (ARM) in the Rivonia trials is not really an example of such resistance in South Africa.

17. *Africa Report* (November 1967), p. 42.

18. *Anti-Apartheid News*, November 1967, p. 1.

19. George Houser, "African Liberation Movements," *Africa Today* Vol. 14, No. 4 (August, 1967), p. 12.

20. George Houser, "African Liberation Movements," *op. cit.*

21. *Ibid.*

22. See "Yankee go Home," *Zimbabwe News*, December 23, 1967, p. 3.

Chapter 7
The Community and the Commonwealth:
Toward New Patterns

1. Zartman, "Africa as a Subordinate State System in International Relations," *International Organization*, Summer 1967.

2. This is the African view. See Balewa, *Nigeria Speaks, op. cit.* p. 92.

3. Zartman, *op. cit.*, p. 550.

4. Michael Brecher, "International Relations and Asian Studies: The Subordinate State System of Southern Asia," *World Politics* (January 1963), p. 220.

5. K. Nkrumah, *I Speak of Freedom*, p. 4. He was one of the first to suggest a Commonwealth Secretariat, giving it more unity and direction. See *West Africa*, July 25, 1964, p. 825.

6. See "Statement by the Government on the Recent Conspiracy," *Ghana Government White Paper*, No. 7/61 (Accra: Government Printers, December 1961), p. 37.

7. *Roundtable*, December 1964, p. 31.

8. See "Whose Club?", *West Africa*, December 25, 1965, p. 1453.

9. Denis Austin, *Britain and South Africa* (London: Oxford University Press), p. 47.

10. *Ibid.*, p. 56.

11. See *Africa Report*, November 8, 1966, p. 26.

12. Philip Neves, *French-Speaking West Africa* (London: Oxford University Press, 1962), p. 80.

13. *Ibid.*, p. 87.

14. Nkrumah was the prime critic. See his speech to the National Assembly, and comment, in the *Evening News*, September 15, 1960, p. 6.

15. P.N.C. Okigbo, *Africa and the Common Market* (Evanston: Northwestern University Press, 1967), pp. 79 and 82.

16. Arnold Rivkin, *Africa and the European Common Market,* 2nd ed. (Denver: GSIS, University of Denver, 1966), pp. 10-13.

17. For details see Rivkin, "The EEC and Africa," *West Africa*, March 11, 1962, p. 269.

18. Thomas Balogh has been one of the most consistent critics of the benefits of the first five-year period. See his article "Africa and the Common Market," *Journal of Common Market Studies*, Vol. 1, No. 1, 1962, pp. 89-90, where he notes that the African nations did not take advantage of the escape clauses of the Rome Treaty "to protect new industries, mainly through a lack of technical knowledge."

19. Okigbo, *op. cit.*, p. 132.

20. *The New York Times*, February 1, 1968, p. 5.

21. This pact provided for certain land rights for the United Kingdom to build military facilities and was negotiated prior to independence. See Claude S. Phillips, *The Development of Nigerian Foreign Policy* (Evanston: Northwestern University Press, 1964), p. 38.

22. William Attwood told the author this. Attwood's book on his "personal adventures" in Africa, *The Reds and the Blacks*, has raised many queries.

23. Chester Crocker, "External Military Assistance to Sub-Saharan Africa," *Africa Today*, April-May, 1968.

24. See Crocker, *Ibid.*

25. See *West Africa,* January 15; 1966, pp. 53-54. *Le Monde* has said France will "judge each case on its own merits."

26. Quoted in "De Gaulle's Warning," *West Africa*, 2357, January 15, 1966, pp. 53-54.

27. Leopold Senghor, *African Socialism, op. cit.,* p. 14.

28. Victor D. Du Bois, "The Search for Unity in French-Speaking Black Africa: Part I," American University Field Staff Reports Service, West Africa Series, Vol. 7, No. 3, June 1965, p. 5.

29. Du Bois, *op. cit.*, "Part III: Mauritania's Disengagement from Black Africa," p. 7.

30. Charles Gallagher, "The Franco-Algerian Agreements: An Analysis of the Policy of Co-operation in Saharan Oil," American University Field Staff Reports Service, North Africa Series, Vol. 11, No. 1, August 1965, p. 8.

Chapter 8
Nonaligned Black Africa and Communist Powers:
Bridge or Battleground?

1. V.I. Lenin, *Imperialism, The Highest Stage of Capitalism: A Popular Outline* (New York: International Publishers, 1939).

2. Dallin, *Soviet Foreign Policy After Stalin*, p. 290.

3. "African Studies in the USSR," *West Africa*, February 15, 1958, p. 151.

4. "The Socialist World System and the National Liberation Movement," *World Marxist Review*, 6 (March 1963), pp. 52-73.

5. A. Lerumo, "Africa Today: Africa's Anti-Imperialist Revolution," *World Marxist Review*, 9 (February 1966), p. 19.

6. Mikhail Kremnyev, "The Non-Aligned Countries and World Politics," *World Marxist Review*, 6 (April 1963), pp. 29-35.

7. Mikhail Kremnyev, *Ibid*.

8. "The USSR and Africa: 1966," *Mizan*, 8, No. 1 (February 1966), p. 40.

9. *20th Conference of the Communist Party of the USSR*.

10. See Richard Lowenthal, "China," in *Africa and the Communist World*, edited by Zbigniew Brzezinski.

11. These points were in summary: 1) equality and mutual benefit; 2) no special privileges; 3) free or low interest loans; 4) self-reliance for recipient development; 5) small investment projects; 6) quality equipment; 7) training of local personnel; 8) Chinese experts living at the local standard. See *Peking Review*, January 31, 1964, p. 9.

12. The extent of Russian penetration of the training of UAR forces after the 1967 Arab-Israel War has gone to the battalion level in the army and the squadron level of the air force. *New York Times*, October 22, 1968, p. 12.

13. "Rethinking the Rail Link," *Africa Today*, Vol. 14, No. 5 (October/November 1967), p. 22. Reprinted from *Business and Economy of Central and East Africa*.

14. The totals for Soviet and Eastern European aid and trade commitments from 1957-1966 are listed in Table 8 of Baard Richard Stokke, *Soviet and Eastern Trade and Aid in Africa* (Praeger Special Studies in International Economics; New York: Frederick A. Praeger, 1967), p. 80. The United Arab Republic, Algeria and Ethiopia have been the primary beneficiaries. Total figures for China are unavailable.

15. The Soviet Union delivered 46,000 tons of oil products to Somalia in 1967. *African Research Bulletin*, February 15 - March 14, 1967, p. 705A.

16. *African Research Bulletin*, March 15 - April 14, 1967, p. 722c.

17. "Friendship between Chinese and African Peoples can Never Be Undermined," *Peking Review*, Vol. 9, No. 3 (January 14, 1966), p. 23.

Chapter 9
The United States and Nonaligned Black Africa

1. Arnold Rivkin, "A View of United States Policy," in Paul F. Power (ed.), *Neutralism and Disengagement* (New York: Scribner Research Anthologies, 1964), pp. 112-113.

2. Arthur Schlesinger points out the significance of Kennedy's priority emphasis on Africa and the acceptance of neutralism in theory as long as it did

not become a vehicle for Communist penetration. "The spread of neutralism neither surprised nor appalled him," *A Thousand Days: John F. Kennedy in the White House* (Boston, Houghton Mifflin Co., 1965), p. 507. Kennedy sought the goal of "a strong Africa," p. 554.

3. James Coleman, "Problems of American Foreign Policy," in *American Government Annual: 1961-62* (New York: Holt, Rinehart & Co.), p. 102.

4. *Ibid.*

5. This positive policy is well described by Rupert Emerson in his *Africa and United States Policy* (Englewood Cliffs, N.J.: Prentice-Hall, 1967), pp. 15-29. For further elaboration, see Schlesinger, *A Thousand Days, op. cit.*, pp. 555-56.

6. George C. Ball *The Discipline of Power* (Boston: Little, Brown, 1968), p. 222.

7. *Ibid.*

8. Rom Landau, *The Moroccan Drama: 1900-1955* (The American Academy of Asian Studies, 1956), p. 212.

9. *In Africa Today*, ed. C. Grove Haines (Baltimore: Johns Hopkins Press, 1955), p. 63.

10. *Ibid.*, pp. 57-59.

11. Gen. S.L.A. Marshall, *South Africa, the Strategic View*, AAAA, November 1967.

12. See Theodore Sorenson, *Kennedy* (New York: Harper & Row, 1964), p. 538.

13. See John Marcum, "Southern Africa and United States Policy: A Consideration of Alternatives," *Africa Today* (October 1967), p. 6.

14. George Ball calls economic sanctions a "romantic delusion," *op. cit.*, p. 245. Charles B. Marshall and Dean Acheson, together with Ball, form the core of a highly influential Washington group of foreign policy advisors opposed to the United Nations sanctions against Rhodesia.

15. Hearings before the Subcommittee on Africa of the Committee on Foreign Affairs, House of Representatives, 89th Congress, 2nd Session, Part 2, Testimony by Nielsen Waldemar, pp. 71-103.

16. Much of this criticism of existing regional integration can be found in Reginald Green and Ann Seidman, *Unity or Poverty: The Economics of Pan-Africanism* (New York: Penguin, 1968), especially pp. 132-170.

17. In an interview between Nicholas B. Katzanbach, then Under Secretary of State, and Sékou Touré, *The New York Times*, May 14, 1967, reported Toure, time and again reiterated that multilateral or regional aid concepts would subject him to economic neocolonialism from France and other European powers.

18. Seventy-seven percent of all United States military aid in Africa has gone to Ethiopia. See Chester Crocker, "External Military Resistance of Sub-Sahara Africa," *Africa Today* (April-May, 1968), p. 18.

19. *The Denver Post*, September 13, 1968, p. 15.

20. *Ibid.*

21. George Ball's proposal of encouraging "enlarged Bantustans" (*op. cit.*, p. 258) is a totally unacceptable alternative.

22. See note 33.

23. See note 32.

24. Gerson, Louis. *The Hyphenate in American Politics and Diplomacy*, University of Kansas Press, p. 238-263.

25. See "Action Notes," and "Afro-Americana," *Africa Today*, September 1968; February-March, 1969.

26. See Stokley Carmichael and Charles Hamilton, *Black Power: The Politics of Liberation in America* (New York: Vintage, 1968), pp. 34-58.

27. An early exposition of this trend is found in "The American Negro Writer and His Roots," selected papers from the First Conference of Negro Writers, March 1959, AMSAC, New York, 1960.

Chapter 10
Nonaligned Black Africa and World Peace

1. General Assembly Plenary Meeting 1352, 7 October 1965, A/PV, 1352.

2. *U.N. Monthly Chronicle*, July 28, 1968, pp. 20-4. Several Asian and Arab states joined in the dissent.

3. There is substantial evidence that President Kennedy's decision not to bomb Cuban missile bases in 1962 was influenced by his concern for the opinion of the world. See especially Robert Kennedy, *Thirteen Days: A Chronical of the Cuban Missile Crisis* (New York: W.W. Norton, 1968).

4. See President Eisenhower's address in Congress, *U.S. Department of State Bulletin,* January 21, 1957, pp. 83-87.

5. See Quaison-Sackey, *Africa Unbound* (New York: Praeger, 1963), p. 117: "The non-aligned states at the United Nations played a decisive role. Mahmoud Riad (of the UAR) and I became their unofficial spokesmen at the Security Council in getting U Thant, Acting Secretary-General, to intervene between the great powers."

6. General Assembly Plenary Meeting, 1144, 5 October 1962, A/PV, 1144.

7. General Assembly Plenary Meeting 1348, 5 October 1965, A/PV, 1348.

8. David A. Kay, "The Impact of African States on the United Nations," *International Organization*, 18 (Winter 1969), pp. 37-39.

9. Quoted in Norman Padelford, *Africa and World Order* (New York: Praeger, 1963), p. 54.

10. Kay, *op. cit.*, p. 41, notes a sharp rise in African abstention on East-West issues.

11. Robert Kennedy, *op. cit.*

12. "Khartoum Liberation Conference," *News Letter,* Institute of Race Relations, January 1969, pp. 37-40.

Index

Index

Abidjan Conference (OCAM, 1965) 88
Accra Heads of State Conference (OAU, 1965), 34, 58, 87
Accra Resolution (1965), 59
Adamafio, Tawia, 97
Addis Ababa Conference (1963), 29, 31
Addis Ababa Council of Ministers Meeting (1964), 58
Adoula, Cyrille, 40, 41, 42, 43, 67
African Development Bank, 32, 36
African Liberation Committee (the Committee of Nine), 32, 67, 72
African National Congress (South Africa, ANC), 64, 70, 71, 72, 73, 96
African Nationalism, 4, 13, 14, 37, 38, 54, 55
African Personality, 14, 18, 23, 36, 116
African Socialism, 7, 8, 21, 66, 87, 116
Afrikaners, 52
"Afro-Asian bloc", 12, 13
Afro-Asian People's Solidarity Organization (AAPSO), 96
Afro-Malagasy Economic Cooperation Organization (OAMCE), 33, 87
Afro-Marxists, 20
Agency for International Development (AID), 109, 117
Ahidjo, Anmadou, 80, 88
Algeria, 19, 20, 21, 26, 27, 28, 34, 72, 73, 98, 101, 103
Algerian Provisional Goverment, 30
Algeiers, Conference (AAPSO), 96
All-African People's Organization (APPO), 12
All-African Trade Union Federation (AATUF), 96
American Committee on Africa, 73
Andrade, Mario de, 68
Angola, 68
Anti-colonialism, 13, 14, 37
Arab League, 26, 31
Arab Socialism, 8
Armée Populaire de Libération (APL), 41, 44
Assimilation, 8, 14, 17
Attwood, William, 102
Austin, Denis, 78

Bafulero, 41
Bakongo, 67
Balewa, Abubakar, 28, 34, 36, 45, 47, 109
Ball, George, 109
Bandung Conference, 12, 96
Bantu states, 26
Barden, A.K., 29

Batetela-Bakusu, 41
Batusa, Kai, 97
Belgium, 38, 44, 45, 46
ben Bella, Ahmed, 23, 94, 127
Benin Union, 33
Biafra, 98, 99
Binza Group, 42
Black Americans, 120, 121
Botswana, 50, 61, 71
Brazzaville Conference (1960), 29
Brazzaville Group, 29, 30, 87
Brecher, Michael, 77
British Commonwealth of Nations, 22, 26, 52, 76, 77, 78, 79, 88, 89
Bureau of African Affairs (Ghana), 29, 72, 97
Busia, Dr. K., 29
Burton, J.W., 3, 5
Burundi, 34, 45, 88, 101

Cabral, Amikar, 67
Cairo Afro-Asian People's Solidarity Conference (1957), 95, 96, 127
Cairo Heads of State Conference (OAU, 1964), 44
Cameroun, 29, 33, 45, 84, 88
Casablanca Conference (1961), 30, 39
Casablanca Group, 28, 30, 31, 39, 42
Central African Federation, 54
Central African Republic, 29, 80, 85, 88, 101
Central Treaty Organization (CENTO), 2, 110
Césaire, Aimé, 24
Chad, 26, 29, 30, 33, 34, 35, 80, 85, 88
Chaliand, Gérard, 67
Chou En-Lai, 95
Cold War, 1, 5, 6, 15, 16, 18, 22, 39, 47, 48, 63, 106, 109, 123
Coleman, James, 19, 20, 108
Colonialism, 13, 14, 18, 22, 26
Comité National de Libération (CNL), 41, 43
Comité Revolucionario de Moçambique (COREMO), 68, 73
Committee for Technical Cooperation in Africa (CCTA), 32
Commonwealth Defense Conference, 79
Communism in Africa, 41, 42, 73, 74, 96, 97, 102, 103, 104
Communist China, 8, 17, 21, 22, 27, 42, 87, 94, 95, 96, 97, 98, 99, 100, 101
Communist Powers, 8, 16, 63, 73, 74, 89, 92, 93, 96, 97, 101

Congo (Brazzaville), 20, 29, 30, 34, 45, 60, 80, 82, 84, 88, 97, 99, 101
Congo (Leopoldville), 31, 56
Congo (Kinshasa), 35, 48, 67, 68, 88, 115
Congo Republic's Army (ANC), 43, 44, 45
Connolly, Admiral Richard L., 110
Conseil de l'Entente, 27, 28, 33, 34, 87
Convention People's Party (CCP), 93, 97
Crabb, Cecil, 5
Cultural Identity, 8, 9, 14, 113, 116
Customs and Economic Union of Central Africa (UDEAC), 27, 28, 82, 114

Daddah, Ould, 87
Dahomey, 27, 29, 33, 88, 101
de Gaulle, Charles, 47, 79, 80, 85
DuBois, W.E.B., 24
Dulles, John Foster, 2, 106

East African Common Market, 82
East African Common Services Organization (EASCO), 24, 26, 27, 28, 36, 114
East African Common Services Organization Treaty (1967), 27
East European countries, 73, 98, 99, 100, 101, 102, 103
Economic and Social Commission (of the OAU), 32
Economic assistance: Communist China, 98, 99, 100, 101; EEC, 82; Great Britain, 81; Soviet Union, 98, 99, 100, 101, 102, 103; United States, 23, 89, 113, 114, 115
Economic diversification, 8, 81, 82, 113
Economic integration, 27, 80, 81, 82, 114, 115
EEC Development Fund, 81
Egypt, 20, 21, 26, 30, 73, 78, 98
English-speaking states, 19, 33, 63, 78, 81, 82, 84, 85, 86, 89
Ethiopia, 15, 35, 45, 63, 99, 113, 115, 124
Ethnic identity, 13
European Common Market (EEC), 16, 22, 27, 28, 33, 79, 80, 81, 82, 89

Fanon, Franz, 13, 64, 65
"Fearless Proposals", 57, 62
Federalism, 28, 29, 31
France, 16, 27, 36-67, 47, 56, 57, 79, 80, 84, 85, 89, 90
Franco-Algerian Oil Agreement (1965), 90
Francophone states, 26, 37, 58, 63, 79, 80, 81, 82, 85, 86, 87

French Community, 76, 79, 80, 84, 88, 89
French-speaking states, 13, 16, 19, 22, 26, 27, 29, 30, 33, 86, 87
Frenta da Libertacao da Mocambique (FRELIMO), 65, 67, 68, 70, 73
Frenta Naçional de Libertacao de Angola (FNLA), 67
Frenta para a Libertacao e Independencia da Guinea Portugesa (FLING), 67
Front of National Liberation (FLN, Algeria), 66
Functionalism, 28, 29, 31

Gabon, 3, 29, 34, 47, 80, 82, 85
Galtung, Johan, 56
Ganao, C.D., 45, 86
Gbenye, Christopher, 41, 42, 43, 44, 94
GENTA, 57
Ghana, 19, 20, 26, 30, 33, 40, 45, 61, 84, 86, 93, 101, 103, 107, 113, 124
Gizenga, Antoine, 40, 42, 43, 86, 94
Goldberg, Arthur, 119
Governo Revolucionario de Angola no Exilio (GRAE), 67, 68, 72, 73
Great Britain, 22, 38, 44-47, 51, 52, 55, 56, 57, 59, 62, 63, 81, 83, 84, 89, 90
Guamane, Paulo, 68
Guinea, 19, 20, 21, 26, 30, 34, 39, 45, 67, 73, 80, 84, 85, 86, 88, 98, 101, 103, 107, 114
Guinea-Bissau, 66, 67

Haile Selassie, 14, 32, 35, 109
Hammerskjuld, Dag, 39
Hassan II, King, 30
Herskovits, Melville, 26
Herter, Christian, 2
Hovet, Thomas, 19
Houphouet-Boigny, Feliz, 26, 29, 33, 79, 87
Houser, George, 73

Ideology, 2, 7, 19, 20, 27
Ikoku, Sam, 97
International Confederation of Free Trade Unions (ICFTU), 97
International Legal Aid and Defence Fund, 73
Intervention: 46, 47; Belgium, 38, 44, 45, 46; Communist China, 95; Communist Powers, 16, 40, 41, 42, 98, 103; France, 36, 37, 47, 85; Great Britain, 38, 44-46, 47, 83; Great Powers, 38, 47-48, 84, 129; Military, 38, 44, 46, 47, 98, 116;

Multi-lateral, 38; United Nations, 38-40; United States, 38, 48, 107, 116; Western Powers, 16, 40, 41, 44-46, 63
Isolationism, 5, 6
Ivory Coast, 27, 33, 58, 84, 88, 94, 114, 124

Japan, 50, 56
Johnson, Lyndon B., 107

Kabaka of Buganda, 47
Kanza, Thomas, 41, 43
Karefa-Smart, John, 125
Kasavubu, Joseph, 31, 39, 40
Katanga, 39, 40, 46
Kaunda, Kenneth, 59, 63
Keita, Modibo, 80, 87, 127
Kennedy, John F., 106, 108, 127
Kenya, 27, 34, 35, 45, 47, 61, 78, 82, 83, 84, 98, 101, 113
Kenyatta, Jomo, 42, 44, 45, 59, 102
Kenyatta Commission, 44, 45, 47
Khama, Seretse, 71
Khartoum Conference, 128
Khrushchev, Nikita, 2, 3, 95
Kimbundu, 68
Kinshasa Heads of State Conference (OAU, 1967), 72
Kitwe United Nations Seminar on Apartheid and Racial Discrimination, 58, 61
Korry Plan, 113
Kremnyew, Mikhail, 94
Kwame Nkrumah Ideological Institute, 97

Lagos Conference (1962), 30
Land Apportionment Act (Rhodesia), 54
Land Husbandry Act (Rhodesia), 54
League of Nations, 6, 57
Legum, Colin, 29, 42, 71
Legum, Margaret, 13, 16
Lenin, V.I., 92
Lerumo, A., 93
Lesotho, 50
Liberation movements, 63, 64, 65, 66, 67, 71, 73
Liberia, 15, 26, 61, 63, 108, 113, 115, 124
Libya, 84, 108, 113, 115
Lissouba, Pascal, 88
Lumumba, Patrice, 30, 39, 40, 41, 42, 98
Lumumba Institute (Nairobi), 102

Madagascar, 84
Maghreb, 26, 28
Malagasy Republic, 29, 34, 80, 86, 88

Malawi, 35, 50, 56, 61, 82, 84, 88
Mali, 19, 20, 26, 27, 30, 33, 34, 39, 56, 80, 83, 84, 85, 86, 88, 98, 101
Mao Tse-Tung, 41, 95
Marshall, General S.L.A., 110
Marxism, 20
Mashona, 52
Matabele, 52, 69
Matthews, Joe, 70
Mauritania, 29, 85, 87, 88, 101
Mazrui, Ali, 15
Mba, Leon, 3, 85
Mboya, Tom, 21
Meany, George, 2, 106
Mercenaries, white, 43, 44, 46
Military ties: 83-85; Communist China, 97-98; France, 84-85; Great Britain, 83-84; Soviet Union, 98; United States, 115-116
Miller, J.D.B., 22
Mobutu, Joseph, 40, 48, 67, 88
Mohammed V. King, 30, 110
Mondlane, Eduardo, 65, 68
Monrovia Conference (1961), 30
Monrovia Group, 28, 30, 31, 39
Morgenthau, Hans J., 7
Morocco, 26, 28, 29, 30, 101, 110, 113, 115
Movement Nationale Congolais (MNC), 40, 43
Movimento Popular de libertacao de Angola (MPLA), 68, 73
Mozambique, 65, 68, 70
Mtshali, B. Vulindlela, 60
Mulele, Pierre, 41
Murumbi, Joseph, 124

Nasser, Gamal Abdel, 6, 15
Negritude, 18, 23, 26, 37, 87
Nehru, Jawaharlal, 2, 6, 15
Neo-colonialism, 3, 18, 20, 21, 24, 38, 80, 85, 86, 93, 94
Neutrality, 5-6
NIBMAR (No Independence Before Majority Rule), 55, 57
Niger, 27, 29, 33, 82, 85, 88
Nigeria, 19, 22, 26, 27, 33, 35, 44, 45, 81, 82, 83, 87, 98, 113, 124
Nigerian Defense Pact, 83
Nkomo, Joshua, 54, 59, 70
Nkrumah, Kwame, 2, 3, 6, 15, 16, 19, 23, 24, 28, 29, 30, 31, 34, 39, 40, 72, 73, 78, 81, 86, 87, 97, 109, 125, 127
North Atlantic Treaty Organization, (NATO), 16, 50, 69, 109, 110-112

Nyerere, Julius, K., 15, 21, 23, 34, 45, 69, 72, 79, 86, 99, 116

Obote, Milton, 47
Odinga, Oginga, 83, 97, 102
Olympio, Sylvanus, 29, 80
Organization of African Unity (OAU) 9, 24, 25, 31-37, 86, 117, 118; Liberation movements, 32, 68, 70, 71-72; UDI, 58-60, 78, Congo Crisis, (1964) 44, 45, 47
Organization Commune Africaine at Malgache (OCAM), 24, 26, 27, 28, 30, 33, 35, 86, 87, 88, 117

Padmore, George, 24
Pan-African Freedom Movement for East, Central and South Africa (PAFMECA), 26
Pan-Africanism, 14, 24-25, 28, 29, 30, 31, 36, 37
Pan-Africanist Congress (PAC), 71, 73
Pan-Negroism, 24
Partido Africano da Independencia da Guinea e Cabo Verde (PAIGC), 67, 33
Peace Corps, 109
Pinto-Bull, 67
POQO, 71
Portugal, 55, 56, 57, 61, 67, 69, 74, 109, 111
Portuguese Guinea, 67, 69
Portuguese Territories, 66-69
"Positive Neutralism", 6, 15, 20, 21, 34
Pritchard, Evans, 26

Race consciousness, 13-14, 62, 74
Race relations, 46, 52-55, 58
Racial attitudes, 52-53
Racial discrimination, 14, 53-54, 55, 58
Racial identity, 37, 95
Racial prejudice, 14, 53
Racism, 14, 18, 45, 53-54, 72
Refugees, political, 34, 41, 66
Regionalism, 33, 36, 37, 114
Rhodes, Cecil, 52
Rhodesia, 35, 50-63, 69-70, 111
Rhodesian Front, 54
Rivkin, Arnold, 106
Roberto, Holden, 67
Rosberg, Carl, 19-20
Rosenau, James, 5, 50
Rwanda, 26, 88

Sabiti, Francois, 43

Sackey, Quaison, 117
Said, Abdul A., 7
Sannequillie Declaration, 30
Scientific, Technical and Research Commission (of the OAU), 32
Segal, Ronald, 17
Senegal, 19, 29, 33, 44, 67, 80, 84, 88, 93, 101, 114
Senghor, Leopold, 18, 26, 34, 80, 82, 87, 116
Shamuyarira, Nathan, 69
Sierra Leone, 61, 84
Simango, Uria, 68
Sithole, Ndabaningi, 59, 69-70
Smith, Ian D., 46, 51, 53, 54, 55, 58
Somalia, 34, 35, 45, 99, 101
Soumialot, Gaston, 41
South Africa, 46, 50, 51, 52, 54, 55, 56, 57, 61, 62, 69, 71-72, 74, 79, 108, 109, 111, 113, 119
South East Asia Treaty Organization (SEATO), 2, 110, 112
Southern Africa, 18, 50, 89, 119
Southwest African National Union, (SWANU), 73
South West African People's Organization (SWAPO), 72, 73
Sovereignty, 7
Soviet Union, 27, 37, 42, 63, 90, 93-94, 96-103
Spear of the Nation, 71
Spiro, Herbert, 4
Sino-Soviet Split, 16, 22, 23
Stanleyville Drop, 20, 34, 38, 44-46, 86, 87
Stanleyville Government (People's Republic of the Congo), 41, 43, 44
Sudan, 26, 34, 35, 40, 42, 51, 60, 78, 84, 97, 98, 99, 101, 113
Subordinate systems, 2, 8, 77, 89
Subordinate systems, white, 50-51, 63, 64, 74
Subsystems, 4, 8, 9, 25
Subsystem(s), nonaligned, 1, 2, 7, 9, 10, 19, 23, 48, 50, 51, 74, 106, 118, 122, 127-129
Subversion, external, 17-18
Subversion, intra-African, 34, 73
Sukarno, Dr. Achmed, 6
Swaziland, 50
Systemic approach, 4-5, 10, 76

Tambo, Oliver, 64
Tananarive Conference (1965), 33
Tanganyika, 27, 42, 76

Tanzania, 20, 22, 26, 27, 47, 58, 59, 60, 61, 70, 72, 73, 79, 82, 83, 84, 86, 97, 99, 101, 124
Tanzania-Zambia rail link, 71, 99, 101, 102
Telli, Diallo, 32
Terrorism Act of 1967 (South Africa), 72
Third World, 1, 22, 122, 127-128
"Tiger Conference", 55
Togo, 29, 33, 34, 88
Toure, Ismael, 96, 97
Toure, Sekou, 20, 23, 26, 29, 67, 79-80, 87, 109
Trade Relations: Communist China, 27, 99, 101; Communist states, 99-101; East European, 101-103; EEC, 81-82; France, 27, 56-57; Great Britain, 56-57, 81; Intra-African, 28, 32, 82; Japan, 56; Soviet Union, 27, 99-101; United States, 27, 113-114
Treaty of Rome (1957), 81
Tshombe, Moise, 40, 42, 43, 45, 46, 67, 88, 107
Tubman, William V.S. 30, 31, 34
Tunisia, 19, 26, 28, 35, 45, 113

U Thant, 39
Uganda, 26, 27, 34, 47, 58, 82, 83, 101
Unilateral Declaration of Independence (UDI), 51-52, 58-59, 69, 78
Union of Africa and Malagasy (UAM), 26, 29, 30, 33, 87
Union of African States of Ghana, Guinea and Mali (UAS), 27, 29
United Arab Republic (UAR), 27, 35, 39, 45, 73, 93, 101, 124
United Nations: 6, 8, 14, 15, 118, 124-125; African states in, 7, 12, 19, 26, 33, 86, 127; Congo crisis, 38-40, 42, 48; Rhodesia, 51, 58-60; sanctions, 56, 57, 60-62, 111
United Nations Conference on Trade and Development (UNCTAD), 125

United Nations Disarmament Commission, 116
United Nations Operation in the Congo (UNOC), 39-40
United States, 23, 27, 37-38, 48, 73- 74, 89-90, 106-109, 112-120
United States Information Agency (USIA), 117
University College of Salisbury, 54
Upper Volta, 27, 29, 33, 45, 85, 88

Welch, Claude, 29
Wellbeck, Nathan, 40
West African Customs Union, 114
West Germany, 56, 111
Western Powers, 48, 63, 65, 73
White Settlers, 52, 53, 57, 64
White supremacy, 18, 65, 71, 119
Whitehead, Sir Edgar, 54
Williams, G. Mennen, 109
Williams, H. Sylvester, 24
Wilson, Harold, 53, 55, 57, 62
World Peace Council, 97
Worsley, Peter, 4

Yameogo, Maurice, 87
Yaounde Agreement (1964), 82
Yifra, Katema, 125
Youlou, Abbe Fulbert, 47, 85

Zambia, 35, 56, 58, 59, 70, 84, 101, 108, 124
Zanzibar, 27, 42
Zartman, I. William, 9, 29, 76
Zimbabwe, 63, 69-71
Zimbabwe African National Liberation Army, 70
Zimbabwe African National Union (ZANU), 69-70, 73
Zimbabwe African People's Union (ZAPU), 54, 69-70, 73

About the Author

George W. Shepherd, Jr. is a professor in the Graduate School of International Studies and the Director of the Center on International Race Relations. He has been the editor of the journal *Africa Today* for the past four years. His previous works include *The Politics of African Nationalism* (1962); *They Wait in Darkness* (1956); *The Racial Impact on American Foreign Relations* (1970). He has taught at African universities, worked with African farmers, traveled widely and published his findings both in Africa as well as the Western world. A charter member of the American Committee on Africa and also a fellow of the African Studies Association, he taught also at Brooklyn College, the University of Minnesota, and The American University. Born in China, he was educated at the University of Michigan and London University.